CROSSING JERUSALEM
AND OTHER PLAYS

Julia Pascal

CROSSING JERUSALEM
YEAR ZERO
THE GOLEM
ST JOAN

OBERON BOOKS

LONDON

First published in 2003 by Oberon Books Ltd.
(incorporating Absolute Classics)
521 Caledonian Road, London N7 9RH
Tel: 020 7607 3637 / Fax: 020 7607 3629
e-mail: oberon.books@btinternet.com
www.oberonbooks.com

A catalogue record for this book is available from the British
Library.

ISBN: 1 84002 361 9

Cover design: Andrzej Klimowski

Printed in Great Britain by Antony Rowe Ltd, Chippenham.

Contents

CROSSING JERUSALEM

to the memory of my father, Cecil Fridjohn
who died in 2002 and who loved Jerusalem

Why I wrote Crossing Jerusalem

I spent most of 2002 writing this play, a year which has been the bloodiest in Israeli and Palestinian post-1948 history. This is not a drama documentary but a fiction rooted in the everyday lives of Israelis and Arabs during the Second Intifada. I decided to set the play in March before the Israeli occupation of Jenin, and when it seemed, wrongly, that life could never be bleaker.

Over the year, I was troubled by the obligation of a playwright to offer a solution and of course this is impossible. My objective in writing this play was to reveal some of the complexities of the situation as lived on the day-to-day level, and also to show that Israeli society is not a homogeneous block, rather a constant debate which remains extremely volatile. Although nobody is religious in this play, of course the Old Testament remains as a fiery background for Israelis and Palestinians. Certainly Abraham's fathering of both Jews and Arabs haunts the territory. Over the several drafts, I explored what it means to be a man, a soldier, a father, a son, a brother, during war. The patriarchal weight of Judaism and Islam is always present. And of course the question of fertility and the bearing of sons, in this context, is highly political.

To root myself in the conflict, I interviewed Palestinians, Lebanese, North Africans, Iraqis, Kurds, Turks and Israelis. Fragments of their lives are in this play. Israelis are still fairly new in British drama. I don't know where the materfamilias Varda came from in my creative process but I know I wanted to create a new type of Jew. (How tired I am of seeing Shylock and Jessica as the major representatives of Jews on the English stage.) I have known many strong Israeli women and their power has impressed me. I once met Shulamit Aloni, the great Jewish lawyer and champion of Arab rights and she was certainly an influence.

I lived briefly in Israel as a teenager and the atmosphere remains a potent energy in my life. The diaspora Jew is connected to the Jewish state and also distanced. I was never in any army. I can't fire a gun. My feelings about being in

Israel were always attraction-repulsion. The repulsion, of which I am not proud, comes from my own horror at meeting my own Middle Eastern identity after my polite English education. I also carry my grandparents' middle-European baggage on my shoulders and these parts of my persona are jostled by the brutal frankness of everyday life in Israel.

And then I am charmed by seeing the international mixture of people who are Jews living in Israel just as I was charmed by my Arab schoolfriends in Jaffa. But, in my naivity, I was also terrified when they told me they would fight the Israelis and me too.

The year spent writing *Crossing Jerusalem* made me explore the deep moral issues discussed in private amongst Jews and certainly many might be offended that I allow these questions to be aired onstage, at this moment, when so many feel vulnerable to a new kind of antisemitism. But self-questioning is a rigorous Talmudic tradition and one which I feel should be allowed onto the British stage. We are disturbed by the idea of building our happiness on someone else's misery. We need to defend but what happens when self-defence brutalises us? Is the Jew to be a 'light unto nations' or is the Jew just like everyone else?

Characters

VARDA KAUFMANN-GOLDSTEIN
a fifty-eight-year-old estate agent

SERGE GOLDSTEIN
her fifty-five-year-old Russian husband

GIDEON KAUFMANN
her thirty-eight-year-old son

LIORA (LEE) KAUFMANN
her thirty-five-year-old daughter

YAEL KAUFMANN
Gideon's thirty-year-old wife

YUSUF KHALLIL
a thirty-year-old Palestinian Muslim

SHARIF KHALLIL
Yusuf's sixteen-year-old brother

SAMMY HADAD
a forty-five-year-old Christian Arab

The play takes place in and near Jerusalem over twenty-four hours at the beginning of March 2002.

Crossing Jerusalem was first performed at the Tricycle, London on 13 March 2003, with the following cast:

VARDA KAUFMANN-GOLDSTEIN, Suzanne Bertish

SERGE GOLDSTEIN, Constantine Gregory

GIDEON KAUFMANN, Adam Levy

LIORA (LEE) KAUFMANN, Miranda Pleasence

YAEL KAUFMANN, Galit Hershkovitz

YUSUF KHALLIL, Nabil Elouahabi

SHARIF KHALLIL, Daniel Ben-Zenou

SAMMY, Jack Raymond

Director, Jack Gold

Assistant Director, Richard Beecham

Designer, Pamela Howard

Lighting Designer, Matthew Eagland

Sound Designer, Crispin Covell

Assistant to Designer, Ada Gadomski

Prologue

Spot on SHARIF.

Sound of tanks, gunfire.

SHARIF: (*Shouting over the noise.*) Hey over there. Get out those bastards over there Remi. Throw like a man Remi. They can't see you. Throw fast, I said fast Remi! Go for it man. You're a kid they can't see you, don't be scared. Throw!
Yes!!! You got one!! Right in the face. You are terrific Remi. And over there, look there are more of the bastards coming. How many can you hit?
Hey look out. The guy over there. On the roof. He's looking right at you. He's aiming right at you. Hey Remi, run man, run.
Blackout.

Scene 1
A Bedroom in a Jerusalem Flat
08:15 hours

Sound of children playing in the street and cars honking their horns.
YAEL and GIDEON are eating a breakfast of bread, olives and cheese in bed.

YAEL: How long do we have?
GIDEON: (*Looks at his watch.*) Eight. Tomorrow at eight.
YAEL: So soon.
GIDEON: Twenty-four hours.
YAEL: Oh it's so short.
GIDEON: You know how it is. Why do you always ask?
YAEL: Longing. Longing to have you for longer.
GIDEON: It's a big day.
YAEL: What?
GIDEON: Today.
YAEL: It's depressing.

GIDEON: Why?

YAEL: The end of youth.

GIDEON: Any more olives?

YAEL: (*Puts some olives from her plate on to his. Beat.*) Could we?

GIDEON: What?

YAEL: You know.

GIDEON: What?

YAEL: Another.

GIDEON: What?

YAEL: You know. (*Points down to her feet.*)

GIDEON: (*Ignoring this.*) Chance of more coffee?
(*YAEL kisses him.*)

YAEL: You taste of toothpaste. (*He kisses her.*) Everywhere.
Touch me everywhere.

GIDEON: Oh you're so demanding and I'm dying of lack
of coffee here! (*GIDEON takes her feet and kisses them.*)

YAEL: Mmm. (*Beat.*) I know. (*Beat.*) Your hands.

GIDEON: What with my hands?

YAEL: You could rub my feet. Obligation. (*She is pushing her
foot into his hands. He rubs it half-heartedly.*)

GIDEON: What?

YAEL: To make love on the sabbath.

GIDEON: Obligation?

YAEL: Blessing from God.

GIDEON: Who's God?

YAEL: And the other foot?

GIDEON: Oh. (*He doesn't rub it.*)

YAEL: You don't like?

GIDEON: And the coffee?

YAEL: How long do we have?

GIDEON: All of today, all of tonight.

YAEL: I want a week.

GIDEON: You know the situation.

YAEL: Where are you going?

GIDEON: Uh oh.

YAEL: I am your wife.

GIDEON: That's why you can't know.

YAEL: And if something happens?

GIDEON: Nothing will happen. Why are you acting this way?

YAEL: Worry.

GIDEON: Stop.

YAEL: (*Stretching.*) The day is ours. And the night.

GIDEON: The day is with my mother. For your birthday.

YAEL: Oh God. Your mother. I forgot.

GIDEON: And Lee may be coming too. I've not seen her in weeks.

YAEL: Anyone else?

GIDEON: You want a party?

YAEL: It's ancient. Thirty.

GIDEON: (*Dryly.*) Yes.

YAEL: It's ancient for a woman having children. How old was your mother when she had you and Lee?

GIDEON: I don't know, how she found the time. She preferred making deals.

YAEL: Does Lee want kids?

GIDEON: How do I know?

YAEL: She always makes me feel like an outsider.

GIDEON: That's crazy.

YAEL: Is that Michaela? (*YAEL listens.*)

GIDEON: Nothing. Out in the courtyard. She's okay. We'll drop her at your mother's later.

YAEL: Okay. (*Beat.*) Maybe she wants a brother.
(*Silence. GIDEON is half asleep.*)

GIDEON: (*Snuggling into half sleep.*) Mm? Avi.

YAEL: Avi? What Avi?

GIDEON: My mouth tastes so sour. Can we drop this?
(*Silence. YAEL is angry.*) Not yet.

YAEL: Why not yet?

GIDEON: Because.

YAEL: Because what?

GIDEON: You think now's a good time?

YAEL: When's a good time?

GIDEON: Wait a bit.

YAEL: I'll be older.

GIDEON: Sarah had a child at ninety.

YAEL: And Abraham fucks the maid. Hello baby Ishmael. Hello the first Arab Jewish war. (*Beat.*) I want another baby now. (*Beat.*) Gideon, the timing's perfect. The fourteenth day.

GIDEON: Perfect for you. Not for me. It's war, Yael. You think that's a good time to bring new children into this hell?

YAEL: I don't understand.

GIDEON: Once I knew a man.

YAEL: Yes.

GIDEON: His wife was pregnant.

YAEL: Yes?

GIDEON: He never came back.

YAEL: Well at least she had something of him.

GIDEON: He was going to be a refusenik.

YAEL: What?

GIDEON: Nothing.

YAEL: Why do you refuse me?

GIDEON: What?

YAEL: You wanted a child, along comes Michaela. I want another, for God's sake I've waited four years and now you say no.

GIDEON: I can't.

YAEL: You deny me.

GIDEON: What?

YAEL: If I were an orthodox woman, I could divorce you for denying me a son.

GIDEON: But you're not.

YAEL: Are you scared?

GIDEON: Scared of what?

YAEL: You tell me. This war?

GIDEON: Scared? No I'm not scared. After what I've seen nothing can scare me.

YAEL: What?

GIDEON: Nothing.

YAEL: What do you mean, what you've seen? (*Silence.*) What have you seen Gideon? (*Beat.*) Why do you never tell me anything? Why do I have to drag stuff out of you. When we first started going together you talked more. Now you never tell me anything.

GIDEON: You want talk. The whole country never stops screaming and yelling and you want more talk?

YAEL: I want a son. (*Silence.*) When Michaela was born I wanted another baby. That minute. And another. She's nearly five Gideon. She's an only child.

GIDEON: Yes.

YAEL: You can't imagine what it's like. You do nothing and the baby grows inside.

GIDEON: (*Pre-occupied.*) Yes.

YAEL: You said you wanted lots.

GIDEON: That was seven years ago.

YAEL: What's changed?

GIDEON: I'm not ready.

YAEL: Ready? What's ready got to do with it? (*Beat.*) If I get pregnant again you will love it.

GIDEON: Oh?

YAEL: You never left me alone. Your hands were all over me even in front of your mother. I think she was jealous. And Lee looked uncomfortable and I didn't give a damn. My body was big and beautiful and so female.

GIDEON: Stop it.

YAEL: Now my breasts ache for a child. Touch them. (*Silence.*) Why do you avoid this? To make new life. It is a wonderful thing.

GIDEON: Yes.

YAEL: You love our daughter?

GIDEON: Of course.

YAEL: You love me?

GIDEON: Of course.

YAEL: You love someone else?

GIDEON: Of course not.

YAEL: You want to make love?

GIDEON: Yael. You only want a baby. I only want you.

YAEL: (*Hits him.*) Then love me now. Let me have what I want now. I want to have someone new come from me, come from us, come from what we do, I want to have

17

someone new who is me, who is you. Our son is longing
to be born. Can't you feel him between us?

GIDEON: I want, I want, I want, is there anything else in
the world apart from what you want?

Scene 2
Varda's Office
12:00 hours

*SERGE is wandering in and out of it, tidying up and putting mail
into envelopes. He is circulating possible buyers with a list of vacant
properties. As he does he whistles from 'Orpheus and Eurydice'.*

VARDA: Yes mother. Okay, I know it's Saturday but no
we're not coming to dinner. That's tomorrow, I told you
yesterday. (*To SERGE.*) Where's that coffee? (*Back to
phone.*) The kids are coming for dinner. Yael's birthday.
What? You just asked me. Tomorrow. (*To SERGE, giving
him a file.*) This house has come up in Petach Tikvah.
Frummer city, why non-frummers want to live there who
knows. (*Back to phone.*) Why can't we come today?
Because we're coming tomorrow. For dinner. So get the
cleaning woman to write it down if you can't remember.
You know how many messages you let for me yesterday?
Twenty-four. That's right. Tomorrow and if you ask me
again I'll throw myself out of the window. Today? No
we're with Yael and Gideon. I just told you. (*To SERGE,
giving him a file.*) Look at this. Twenty-five apartments.
I've got to get this finalised.

SERGE: Oh?

VARDA: Didn't I mention?

SERGE: Twenty-five apartments?

VARDA: Yes.

SERGE: Twenty-five?

VARDA: So?

SERGE: What about the money? (*Gives her a coffee.*)

VARDA: (*Looking through files.*) Oh God there are so many
people involved. The Kleins from Paris. Every day they

call. Between Le Pen and the Arabs, they've had enough
of France.

SERGE: The money?

VARDA: (*Back to phone.*) Yes I'm here mother. And Gideon's
coming over. Not in the car. I tell him don't drive across
town. We walk now. We walk real fast. Tomorrow mother,
tomorrow. (*She hangs up.*)

SERGE: Varda?

VARDA: Yes?

SERGE: You're avoiding the question.

VARDA: What question?

SERGE: The money. How will you find enough?

VARDA: I'm waiting for a loan. Today. Please God they call
me today or I could lose the whole deal. And there's this
problem with the tree.

SERGE: A tree? What's with a tree?

VARDA: They say the roots are growing underneath. How
can a tree make a whole building crumble? It's a fantasy.
Then they ask us to get the mayor to give us permission
to get the tree removed. Are they crazy? (*Beat.*) Oh God,
there are half cups of coffee all over the office. I'm a slut.
Clean them up will you. And all this mail, get me some
stamps will you.
(*Sound of the Muslim mid-morning call to prayer in the
distance.*)

SERGE: I'm not your secretary, Varda.

VARDA: I told them it's urgent. Call me anytime.

SERGE: You're driving me crazy with this loan. I don't
understand how it works. How will you pay it back?

VARDA: It's money for nothing.

SERGE: For nothing?

VARDA: I loan, I rent. Money coming in is five times
money going out. It's important. It's the biggest deal I've
ever pulled. We can relax afterwards. Retire on the profit.

SERGE: Maybe you're borrowing too much? You can't be
sure you'll make profit.

VARDA: Don't depress me. Why do you always try and pull
me down. Isn't it hard enough? And I have to do the
whole damned thing on my own. Everyone thinks it's so

19

easy you just pick up the phone. They don't know all the work that's behind.

SERGE: I know, I know.

VARDA: And that girl Gideon married, you know what, she asked me to babysit Michaela last week. As if I have nothing else to do.

SERGE: What about Yael? Can she help you here?

VARDA: You kill me. Yael? What does she know about business! Can you see her running to the bank and discussing cash-flow with the manager or taking clients around the apartments? She's in a dream world, that girl. She never helps Gideon with his business, she could. I don't know why he married her.

SERGE: She's okay.

VARDA: As long as a girl's pretty, for you, she's okay. But what's inside the head, tell me that. And what family is she from. The mother speaks Arabic better than she speaks Hebrew.

SERGE: Varda!

VARDA: And Gideon's no better. What did I do that was so wrong? Both my kids such a mess. You know when they're small, you think they'll be exceptional people. Then they grow up and they're just like everyone else.

SERGE: Sorry about that.

VARDA: And Lee not married yet. She's thirty-five and not even serious with anyone except for that old cock Jake. My eyes are so sore, why are they so sore? Maybe it's glaucoma. I'm scared to go to the optician and get the pressure tested.

SERGE: Am I what you thought?

VARDA: You? What do you mean? You?

SERGE: After Heiner, am I what you expected?

VARDA: Heiner, Heiner. Sometimes it was shit with Heiner. (*Beat.*) But now I'm going crazy and you don't help.

SERGE: Is that where the money's coming from?

VARDA: What?

SERGE: Heiner's money.

VARDA: I need to get it out of the investment bond and it could cover some of the loan, yes.

SERGE: Why didn't you tell me?

VARDA: You're awful with money.

SERGE: Where did Heiner get money?

VARDA: Reparations. His grandparents were German Jews. Auschwitz.

SERGE: I never knew.

VARDA: They paid Heiner's parents and it ended up with Heiner and he said to keep it for the kids. Well I invested it and now it's going to part-pay the loan.

SERGE: How much?

VARDA: A third.

SERGE: And the other two thirds?

VARDA: Stop worrying.

SERGE: I'm only worrying for you. (*Beat.*) I wish I could make money but what can I do?

VARDA: Serguei. Serguei. Who would know how any of this would turn out? (*Beat.*) Make me a coffee will you.

SERGE: What's that in your hands?

VARDA: I'm off the planet. Let me tell you Serguei, I am seriously worried. Even if I get the loan that tree will hold up the sale. And if the town council won't let us get rid of the tree we can't sell. And okay people still want to buy in Jerusalem but every time some Arab blows himself up it feels like the world will end. Why don't I have Alzheimer's like mother? The perfect Jewish disease.

SERGE: Why don't we invite your mother today?

VARDA: Are you crazy? (*Beat.*) But you know sometimes she talks sense. My mother, she says, 'Old people, they shouldn't be born.' She says, 'When you get old even shitting's work.'

SERGE: We could go to the US. Or you want me to take you back to Russia? Believe me it's worse there. Let's try New York.

VARDA: We should run away?

SERGE: Don't you like New York?

VARDA: In the Second Avenue Deli, I burst into tears. Like walking into my grandparents' house. Even the waitress spoke Yiddish.

SERGE: So what's the problem?

VARDA: You left Russia to come here. Don't you understand?

SERGE: Or Europe?

VARDA: You think I don't have these thoughts too?

SERGE: France?

VARDA: This is our country. If it goes to hell then we'll go with it.

SERGE: Varda, I'm scared for you every time you go out the door.

VARDA: And then someone calls. 'Find me an apartment. For my wife. My kids.' And I get them a place. They come here from Paris and London and I make them happy. That's my job. They come here. I don't want to go there. (*Beat.*)

Don't you get it, Serguei? Russians, Americans, French, all those Jews who want to come in. I house them. I visit them, sitting in their garden, there's the sound of the crickets and they are there, eating dinner as the sun drops into the sea. They sit on their balcony cutting water melon and letting the red luscious flesh fill their mouths and they know that now they really are in Israel. They're not afraid to say, 'I am a Jew.' They don't have to hear church bells or see a man hanging from a cross and the world is not drunk for two weeks. Here they are Jews in their own country. Here they don't need to hide who they are. And I help them. I love it.

SERGE: California?

(*The buzzer rings.*)

VARDA: Get that will you.

SERGE: Yes madam.

(*SERGE leaves, whistling. Sound of children playing. GIDEON enters.*)

VARDA: Do you have to whistle all the time? Oh it's you. I've been calling your cell for hours.

GIDEON: I turned it off.

VARDA: Why do you do that? I hate it.

GIDEON: Peace sometime would be nice.

(*Outside. Sound of a helicopter. Sound of whistling.*)

VARDA: I'm sweating with fear, you don't call. It's twelve noon or haven't you got a watch?

GIDEON: You said to be in the apartment for eleven. You weren't home. I walked over.

(*LEE enters.*)

VARDA: You're right I'm losing it.

LEE: Hi mother.

VARDA: And what are you wearing?

LEE: What am I wearing? What am I wearing? What does it look like I'm wearing?

VARDA: You forget your skirt?

LEE: It's the fashion.

VARDA: Yael's birthday. You could have worn a dress.

LEE: Where's Yael?

GIDEON: In a few minutes.

(*SERGE enters.*)

VARDA: Does she know where you are? Does anyone tell her where you are?

GIDEON: Calm down, will you.

LEE: Tomorrow I go to the army.

GIDEON: Oh.

VARDA: That means both of you on reserve at the same time. Are they allowed to do that?

LEE: I'm safe don't worry. The medical unit is safe.

VARDA: Safe? (*Beat.*) You come for her birthday like that?

LEE: You want me to go home and change?

VARDA: Your sister. She's always going out with older men.

LEE: Please.

VARDA: Old men have weak sperm.

(*SERGE enters.*)

SERGE: Really?

LEE: Jake's not that old.

VARDA: Time I had a grandson. Everyone I know has grandsons, why do I have to be different? And now this one. Jake. Twenty years older than the last. He's divorced. He's got kids already. You want a father or a husband? She comes here during the week and all the men they fall for her. Your sister, she can have any man she wants. What does she do, she picks the oldest. 'Jake's my new partner!'

GIDEON: Is that the guy I met here last time? Is that the guy you're with now?

VARDA: What can I say. I can't say anything, what can I say, leave my daughter alone. You're too old? He's my age.

SERGE: Why is everyone in such a bad mood? Sorry about that. (*SERGE starts to whistle again.*)

VARDA: You know at your age hormones start to change. You never know how early the menopause starts. With some women it's even at thirty. Did you go for that smear test like I told you?

LEE: For God's sake.

VARDA: You want a child at sixty. That's what's happening now. Sixty-year-old women, can you believe it?

LEE: You carry on like this and I'm going home.

SERGE: All I want is everyone gets married. Big weddings. Big barmitzvahs. Pity they don't need an accordion at funerals. I'd be a millionaire. Sorry about that.

GIDEON: Any chance of a drink here?

SERGE: I had a business as a musician and then they blew up the wedding hall. I had a business as a taxi driver and now there's no tourists to drive. I cooked in a Russian restaurant and now nobody goes to restaurants. I've run out of jobs. Sorry about that.

VARDA: Where's Yael?

GIDEON: She's coming.

SERGE: And when did this all start?

LEE: Nineteen sixty-seven.

VARDA: For how much longer we fight this Six Day War? Forty years? Fifty?

SERGE: Until there are thirty-six wise men on the earth.

LEE: What?

GIDEON: You might as well wait for the Messiah.

SERGE: A strong fist the Arab understands. And respects.

LEE: Yes Comrade Stalin.

SERGE: Stalin was a monster. You think I'm a monster? I had a son killed in Afghanistan. I know about this.

LEE: Sorry about that.

GIDEON: They're not Arabs in Afghanistan.

VARDA: I read the Taliban were once a Jewish tribe. Maybe the whole world's Jewish, that's why it's such a mess. I even read that Elvis Presley had a Jewish grandmother.

SERGE: And David Beckham. And the mother of Leonardo da Vinci!

LEE: What?

SERGE: That bar mitzvah. In Yossi's dance hall. They were all Russians.

VARDA: Oh God and I don't have enough food.

SERGE: Yossi he just walks up and down the empty wreck of a dance hall. Everyday. Still looking for his brother.

LEE: What?

SERGE: Everyone just eating. Very slow. The noise, I thought it was a firecracker. In the air, legs and arms flying all over. And these people, two minutes before, they were whole and they were dancing. And I was playing. And now there was only screaming and blood all over me.

VARDA: It happened. It happened. Do you have to keep talking about it?

SERGE: From Moscow. To Israel. Nothing they bring. Only their lives.

VARDA: I said stop it.

SERGE: The accordion, better than a bullet-proof vest.

LEE: The accordion?

VARDA: You told me a million times.

SERGE: And all that waiting for Communism to end. Finally Yossi and his brother, they come to Israel.

VARDA: I know. I know. I know.

SERGE: And that's it. His brother. Just standing there. Hurting nobody.

GIDEON: What about the birthday meal. Can I at least get some champagne?

VARDA: Oh God, I invite you to eat and he tells me, 'Don't go to the supermarket unless you want to die.'

SERGE: Sorry about that. (*He finds some pistachio nuts. He cracks them open and eats.*)

VARDA: How can I make lunch if there's no food? There's no food in the apartment. (*To SERGE.*) Can you find my watch? I wanted to go shopping yesterday morning. In the market. He says don't go to the market they'll blow it up. What am I supposed to do, grow vegetables in window boxes?

SERGE: We go out to eat. We cross Jerusalem. Sammy's.

VARDA: You crazy?

LEE: It's a good idea. There's nothing to eat here. (*She takes some nuts from SERGE.*)

VARDA: Jerusalem will soon be Hamas City. Let the Palestinians save their bombs. If they dig a hole and throw me in it can't be too soon.
(*Her mobile rings.*)
Yes, yes Mrs Weiner.
(*LEE's phone rings.*)
Only two bedrooms, nothing bigger.

LEE: (*On the phone.*) Not now. I told you last night.

SERGE: I saw a taxi this morning.

VARDA: Not Haifa. Not Jerusalem. Maybe Netanya.
Serguei, can you find my watch?

SERGE: He draws up to another taxi.

GIDEON: You want a vodka?

SERGE: Hey Moshe! I've got a tourist!

LEE: What do you want of me? I told you not this week.

VARDA: He calls night and day. He doesn't trust you? Why is Yael so late?

LEE: You don't own me, Danny.

VARDA: Who's Danny?

LEE: I told you no. (*To VARDA.*) I'm talking mother.

VARDA: In my own office I'll shut up. (*To phone.*) Mrs Wiener, listen, when you get to Tel Aviv, call me. (*To SERGE.*) Did you find it?

LEE: Next week. I'll call you next week.
(*Sound of sirens in the distance.*)

SERGE: Look at him. He's hungry.

GIDEON: I'm not hungry. I could do with a drink.

SERGE: Well I'm hungry. (*Eating nuts.*) Here's your watch. When is your late wife coming?

GIDEON: Stop worrying.

LEE: How long have you got?

GIDEON: Eight in the morning.

LEE: Me too.

VARDA: I'll make you a sandwich. There's herring in the fridge. And bread.

GIDEON: I don't want to eat.

LEE: Is that what we're doing for Yael's birthday.

VARDA: I'll make. I'll make. (*VARDA leaves.*)

LEE: Herring on ry. A

SERGE: I have such pain in my toes.

LEE: Oh?

SERGE: Only when I walk.

LEE: Is this new?

SERGE: Some days it's okay.

LEE: Oh?

SERGE: Other days every step is agony.

LEE: Did you see a doctor?

SERGE: I'm scared.

LEE: Scared?

SERGE: I lost a son in Afghanistan and now I'm scared to go to the doctor.

LEE: Arthritis?

SERGE: Suddenly my toes hurt and I'm an old man.

LEE: What does Varda say?

SERGE: I don't tell Varda.

LEE: Oh?

SERGE: Between husband and wife you can't imagine what's not said. (*Beat.*) Sorry about that. Forget it. Okay, if we're not eating soon, I'm going outside for a smoke. (*SERGE leaves; silence.*)

LEE: What is it? You look awful.

GIDEON: Do I?

LEE: How's Yael?

GIDEON: Yael's fine. Everything's fine.

LEE: And the office?

GIDEON: Who wants graphic designers when we are at war.

LEE: Is that why you're down?

GIDEON: No.

LEE: So what is it?

GIDEON: Nothing.

LEE: Come on.

GIDEON: Nothing.

LEE: Gideon.

GIDEON: I said nothing.

LEE: I'm your sister.

GIDEON: Nothing. Just tired.

LEE: Tired?

GIDEON: Problems sleeping.

LEE: Why?

GIDEON: The heat.

LEE: The heat?

GIDEON: Yeh. (*Beat.*) You think those refuseniks...

LEE: What?

GIDEON: Got it right?

LEE: I don't know.

GIDEON: They've got guts. I haven't.

LEE: What do you mean?

GIDEON: Refusing to go to the territories.

LEE: You know it's not so simple.

GIDEON: I'm going to the territories. Tomorrow. (*Beat.*)
I shouldn't be telling you.

LEE: I wouldn't guess?

GIDEON: 'Peace and love man.' All our childhood. And
now they want us to clean up all this crap.

LEE: They were naive.

GIDEON: That first day, in the army. Eighteen. I put on the
uniform and I caught myself in a mirror. (*Silence.*) There
was a man looking back at me. Lee I don't think I can go
there anymore. Suppose we keep Jerusalem and give
back the territories?

LEE: The Arabs want the lot. Wouldn't you?

GIDEON: Want, want want, everybody wants.

LEE: We don't exist. On Arab maps there is no Israel.

GIDEON: And where in our heads is Palestine? (*Beat.*) Got
a cigarette?

LEE: No.

GIDEON: Maybe Serge has a cigarette for me.

LEE: Who do you talk to when you're down?

GIDEON: Talk to?

LEE: Everyone has someone they talk to.

GIDEON: Do they?

LEE: I always felt I could tell you anything.

GIDEON: You can. What's bothering you?

LEE: You like Jake?

GIDEON: I hardly know him. I said hello once or twice. Is this IT?

LEE: Well yes. And no.

GIDEON: Meaning?

LEE: I'm not really with him.

GIDEON: What?

LEE: Well I see him.

GIDEON: And?

LEE: I see him and…

GIDEON: And what?

LEE: Other guys.

GIDEON: Oh.

LEE: She doesn't know.

GIDEON: Yes.

LEE: I let her go on thinking it's just Jake.

GIDEON: She hates that you go with him.

LEE: Yes. When I am with him I think how much she hates him and that turns me on.

GIDEON: Oh.

LEE: It's hard *not* to be fucked out there.

GIDEON: What?

LEE: When you're doing it with one man, there are always others who get interested.

GIDEON: Yeh?

LEE: Like they smell you.

GIDEON: Mmm?

LEE: I leave one guy and you know.

GIDEON: What?

LEE: A car comes up or a guy stops in the street.

29

GIDEON: And?

LEE: Sometimes I...

GIDEON: What?

LEE: It shocks you?

GIDEON: What do you do?

LEE: You know.

GIDEON: Oh.

LEE: I go out. With friends or alone. For a walk, for a talk, for a drink.

GIDEON: And?

LEE: I wait till I get a certain look.

GIDEON: A look?

LEE: A look that burns a hole in my belly. You ever get that?

GIDEON: What?

LEE: That hot feeling.

GIDEON: I don't know.

LEE: He's got to be cute.

GIDEON: Cute?

LEE: And smart.

GIDEON: You have time to find this out?

LEE: Over a drink, yes.

GIDEON: Well.

LEE: That feeling.

GIDEON: Yes.

LEE: I can't live without it.

GIDEON: Yes.

LEE: Something to do with being here.

GIDEON: What?

LEE: Jerusalem. The fucking dying capital of the world.

GIDEON: Yeh.

LEE: Just so you know.

GIDEON: Yeh.

LEE: (*Beat.*) We stood up in our beds, in our white sheets, to make wedding dresses. We promised to get married. Remember?

GIDEON: Yeh.

LEE: Did you ever tell anyone?

GIDEON: Who would I tell?

LEE: When I was helping in school this morning.

GIDEON: Mm?

LEE: With Esther in the drop-out school sometimes.

GIDEON: You still do that? Jews and Arabs. You think that's going to work?

LEE: Yeh.

GIDEON: Why bother?

LEE: I am naive. I am stupid. I still have hope.

GIDEON: I'm just dead.

LEE: Jamil, he's maybe seventeen. He asks me really politely, 'Please Miss, can I go home at eleven?'

GIDEON: There used to be whisky here.

LEE: I say, 'Why, why do you want to go home in the middle of the morning?'

GIDEON: She used to have whisky here.

LEE: He says, 'I have to throw stones at the soldiers.'

GIDEON: The bitch.

LEE: And then when there's a suicide bomb in Jerusalem, these Arab kids who throw stones, they call me up and ask, 'You okay Miss?'

GIDEON: Is there really no whisky in this place?

LEE: Can you believe that? Jamil, he doesn't even want to live in Palestine. He hates the United States but wants to live in New York. He wants to have Nike shoes and eat McDonalds. But still he throws stones. (*VARDA enters with a tray full of herring on rye with garnishes.*)

VARDA: Where's Serge now?

LEE: Smoking on the balcony.

VARDA: One husband dies with lung cancer I need two? (*Yells.*) Serge!
(*Enter YAEL.*)

YAEL: I'm late. I'm sorry. Hello mother. The door was open. (*Kisses her.*)

VARDA: The door was open? (*Yelling.*) Serge what are you thinking!

SERGE: (*Entering.*) I thought I smelt food.

VARDA: Late, late this girl is always late. Nice dress. Was it expensive?

31

LEE: Happy birthday.

SERGE: What a beautiful girl – happy birthday darling. (*Kisses her.*)

YAEL: I'm late because I was looking at my emails. 'Send a message to six million Jews before Passover.' Imagine that.

VARDA: How can you find six million Jews?

YAEL: You send to all your friends who send to all their friends and, little by little, you hope that six million names are on the list.

SERGE: I got an email today.

VARDA: Oh?

SERGE: 'Messiah decides not to come to Jerusalem. Parents worried for his safety.' (*Beat.*) It's not all bad. Sales of anti-depressants are going up.

VARDA: Last night I had such a pain in my head, I thought I'd take a long hot bath to get rid of it. Then I realised I already was in a long hot bath.

YAEL: I'm hungry.

SERGE: I hear at Sammy's they give free hummus to any Jews who dare to eat there. That's a cheap meal.

YAEL: We got engaged in Sammy's.

VARDA: I didn't know that.

SERGE: Varda, your son doesn't tell you everything. There's another woman in his life now.

LEE: Let's go.

VARDA: Crossing Jerusalem. You all want to be blown to bits?

YAEL: Suddenly in Sammy's he says, let's get married.

VARDA: They poison our food.

GIDEON: What?

VARDA: Didn't you hear what's happening?

LEE: It happens. But not at Sammy's. He's a Christian Arab.

VARDA: But who do they hire for the kitchen?

SERGE: Varda stop now.

VARDA: You go, you go without me. What is it with you? You forbid me to go shopping and now you want to drive us all to an Arab town to be poisoned or blown up?

SERGE: It's in Israel.

VARDA: You don't let me go shopping but it's okay to cross
Jerusalem?

SERGE: We can't live like dead people.

VARDA: You haven't spent your whole life here. You don't
know what it's been like. We trusted them. We had them
in our homes. And now, after all we offered them, look
what's happening. Soon we're going to have no country
at all.

SERGE: Sorry about that.

GIDEON: That's what the Palestinians have. No country.

VARDA: I thought they have twenty-two.

SERGE: You're frightened. It's normal. We're all frightened.

YAEL: It's my birthday. I'm thirty years old. Thirty years.
And you think we can just go out and get something
decent to eat?

SERGE: We go to Sammy's. We cross Jerusalem. What do
you say?

GIDEON: I want us all to be together and to try and be
happy one day a year. I say Serge is right. What do you
say?

LEE: Fine with me.

SERGE: Well Varda?

VARDA: You want me to die. You all want me to die?

Scene 3
Sammy's Restaurant
14:00 hours

*YUSUF is cutting vegetables. There is Arabic music playing. YUSUF
is swaying to the music. SAMMY comes in to check the till. He moves
to the music as he walks through the restaurant and then leaves.
SHARIF enters.*

SHARIF: Blew the kid's fucking head off.

YUSUF: What?

SHARIF: Before sunrise.

YUSUF: What?

SHARIF: Remi. Twelve years old.

YUSUF: Shit.

SHARIF: For what? For throwing stones.

YUSUF: Yeh.

SHARIF: Is that all you can say to me? Yeh?

YUSUF: Why did you have to go out there?

SHARIF: You want me to sit inside and do nothing?

YUSUF: Why do you go out? You are killing our mother.

SHARIF: I'll stay home, help her wash dishes.

YUSUF: Better than looking for trouble.

SHARIF: Looking for trouble? Is that how you see it? Looking for trouble? You make me sick.

YUSUF: And you want to be the kid with his head blown off? Is that what you want?

SHARIF: You understand nothing.

YUSUF: Is that what you think?

SHARIF: You're too old. You're not with the kids on the street

YUSUF: You dare to talk to me like that?

SHARIF: It's the truth.

YUSUF: I give up. I try to please them. I try to please you. I have to make some money. Everything I do turns to sand.

SHARIF: You don't know what it's like.

YUSUF: What?

SHARIF: When I am out there. When I am fighting. I feel my whole body excited. My heart, it beats in my mouth. Everything about me is beating.

YUSUF: I can't even tell them where you are at night. And you're excited! You get off on war and they'll kill you and fuck it you are my kid brother.

SHARIF: I am a man.

YUSUF: Sixteen. It's nothing.

SHARIF: Nothing. Is that what you think of me?

YUSUF: I didn't say that.

SHARIF: I've seen more than you'll ever see.

YUSUF: And what does that mean?

SHARIF: Nothing.

YUSUF: Go home.

SHARIF: I said no.

YUSUF: Where do you go? Who do you see?

SHARIF: Are you my keeper?

YUSUF: Yes.

SHARIF: And why?

YUSUF: I am your brother and you will obey me.

SHARIF: Remi was more of a brother to me.

YUSUF: How dare you.

SHARIF: He's dead. And you make salads for the Jews.

YUSUF: Our father sweated his guts out to send his sons to Beir Zeit.

SHARIF: How many times do I have to hear this. Go to Beir Zeit and get a degree!

YUSUF: And there was only money for me. How do you think that makes me feel?

SHARIF: Beir Zeit is closed. Beir Zeit is shot to pieces. Beir Zeit is a graveyard for clever Arab boys.

YUSUF: You think I like working here? You think I like washing dishes? I should have been at Beir Zeit. I should be an engineer. You want me to be a martyr then you'd love me like you love Remi. (*Silence.*) Don't you ever think of our parents?

SHARIF: Every night my pillow is soaked with tears.

YUSUF: You should be there.

SHARIF: I'll get roses sent round.

YUSUF: Some respect.

SHARIF: Respect? I've got respect.

YUSUF: Every night they ask me about you. At breakfast they set your place but you never come.

SHARIF: What do you want from me?

YUSUF: You should be in school. What do you learn? Nothing?

SHARIF: What school? I was in school with Remi. I just want to go out there and kill them like they kill us.

YUSUF: I know that. You think I don't want to kill them too. But bodies and bodies and bodies. Is that the answer? Fuck it man is it too much to want you safe?

SHARIF: Safe? Safe? Safe is dead.

YUSUF: What?

SHARIF: I have a dream.

(*An alarm goes off in the distance.*)

SHARIF: I don't need to sleep. It just comes in here. (*Taps head.*) I am walking through Jerusalem and there isn't a Jew in sight. No guys in big hats and beards. No boys in the army. No girls in the army. No guns. Isn't that something? No guns anywhere? And as I walk, I am suddenly in Tel Aviv. In Jaffa. In Ashkelon. In Beer Sheva. Everywhere and not a single Jew. Imagine. No Jews at all. No Hebrew lettering, no Hebrew radio or television, no sound of their spat-out language. No Israeli jets. No jeeps. No road blocks. No queues waiting. No tanks. No noise. No screaming. It is quiet. They are gone. Just like all those other empires that have been in Jerusalem. There is only us. When I have this in my head then I feel this amazing happiness as if I am sky walking over Jerusalem. Over the Old City. I am sky walking over our fields, our olive groves. I am walking through air. I don't know how. You ever do that?

YUSUF: I never dream.

SHARIF: And then I wake up. And they blew Remi's head off. How do I forget the kid's head shot off? Tell me that big man. (*Beat.*) They got the Israeli soldiers and they tore them to pieces. And they stood at the window showing their hands with the Israeli soldiers' blood. You know, those soldiers, they just got lost, they wandered into our area and they ended up dead. And when I saw those hands and when I knew the Jews were dead, I wanted to sing. I wanted to dance.

(*Enter SERGE. SHARIF and SERGE look at one another. SHARIF makes to leave.*)

YUSUF: I want you back here. Before five. Do you hear me?

SERGE: Hi Sammy.

SAMMY: (*Placing SERGE.*) Moscow. That's it. Brezhnev, Gorbachev, Putin. Long time since you've been around.

Your wife, isn't she selling houses and you, you used to bring me customers. In your taxi.

SERGE: I've four hungry people outside. Can I bring them in?

SAMMY: You made a reservation?

SERGE: Suddenly you're the Ritz?

SAMMY: A wedding party in an hour. Forty people.

SERGE: Oh God. I've parked them down the hill. You mean I have to walk ten minutes to tell them they can't eat here.

SAMMY: Should've booked.

SERGE: My wife was jumpy crossing Jerusalem. She didn't even want to have the car outside your place and if I go back and say there's no space, she'll have a stroke.

SAMMY: You want a vodka? Serge isn't it? You want a cigar?

SERGE: You're a generous man.

SAMMY: (*Giving cigar.*) Look at that. From Cuba. Now there's a country!

SERGE: The Communists, you like the Communists?

SAMMY: You like the cigar?

SERGE: (*Taking it.*) Sorry about that. (*Beat.*) My daughter in law. It's her birthday today.

SAMMY: Congratulations.

SERGE: And you, how've you been?

SAMMY: I work. I sleep. I make love to my wife.

SERGE: Only your wife?

SAMMY: She'd divorce me.

SERGE: So many beautiful girls here. It's not the same as in Russia. The way they walk. The way they look you straight in the eye. So arrogant it drives me crazy. And their bottoms. You see the whole world in their arse.

SAMMY: Yeh.

SERGE: Suddenly I got old. I look at them. Now they don't even see me.

SAMMY: I wouldn't have the time.

SERGE: Time. Time. Suddenly, for the first time since I've been in this country there's time. (*Beat.*)

SAMMY: You should've called. (*Gives him a plate of hummus and bread.*)

SERGE: My daughter in law.

SAMMY: She's beautiful?

SERGE: Of course she's beautiful.

SAMMY: Ah. (*Indicates the table.*)

SERGE: She's beautiful and suddenly you got space?

SAMMY: A man can look.

SERGE: Tits and ass and suddenly you got space? (*Beat.*) This Jewish violin student Abe, he goes to heaven and God says, 'Show me what you can do.' So Abe says, 'You gotta violin?' God says, 'No violins here.' So Abe says, 'You gotta piano?' God says, 'No, no piano.' Abe says, 'So how can I show you what I do?' God sits him down by a table and says, 'Here, pretend this is a piano.' Abe raises his hands above the table, he's about to play when God says, 'Hold it, hold it. Already too loud!'

SAMMY: I heard it already.

SERGE: Sorry about that.

SAMMY: You like the hummus?

SERGE: Hummus is hummus.

SAMMY: Don't insult me. Is one woman like another? Taste and texture and care, all that goes into making a woman beautiful. The same goes for hummus. The mix, it should be right.

SERGE: Hummus, women. That's how simple it should be.

SAMMY: Eat. Eat. You're not eating. What is it? You get better hummus where you come from?

SERGE: You became my mother?

(*SAMMY pours them both a vodka. SAMMY feels the bottle.*)
I like you put it in the freezer.

SAMMY: I heard once that a man who had an accident, he survived in the snow, freezing saved him.

SERGE: Have you ever been to a morgue?

SAMMY: A morgue?

SERGE: My father, when I was ten, he took me to a mortuary.

SAMMY: What kind of father was that?

SERGE: He was a doctor. (*Beat.*) I saw this man.
　　Completely blue. I never forgot. (*Drinks.*) Varda always
　　leaves it out. Drives me nuts. What is it with women.
　　One simple thing you ask, they ignore you. My first wife
　　was the same.

SAMMY: How many wives you got?

SERGE: Masha, was number one. An aeronautical engineer.
　　Very smart at work. Very dumb at home. Divorce.
　　(*Looking at his watch and stubbing out his cigar. He waves air
　　around himself to hide the tobacco smell.*) Shit, divorce is
　　what I'll get now if I don't get back out there. (*Beat.*)
　　This place. It's not booked at all. Is it? Meschugennah.
　　(*SAMMY motions to bring the others in. SERGE leaves.
　　YUSUF bangs his fist into his palm three times.*)

SAMMY: What's wrong with you?

SERGE: My brother. I don't know what he'll do. I'm scared.
　　I'm useless.

SAMMY: You are a good kid. You could be my son but God
　　cursed me with only daughters. The eldest's getting
　　married next month. Two hundred people. Her mother's
　　going crazy with the whole affair. Women, they love
　　weddings but for the father it's only expense and more
　　expense. (*Silence.*)

YUSUF: How much is the wedding?

SAMMY: I had to remortgage the whole restaurant.

YUSUF: How much?

SAMMY: More than your dreams. We're setting five.

YUSUF: You know what I think.

SAMMY: Mm?

YUSUF: It's all shit. Whatever I try turns to shit. (*Beat.*)
　　Now you, well you do well. No matter what shit's going
　　on you do alright.

SAMMY: Business.

YUSUF: You sell your soul for business.

SAMMY: Sell my soul. Is that how you see it? Then it can't
　　be worth much.

YUSUF: Some might call it collaboration. Christians and
　　Jews.

SAMMY: What?

YUSUF: There are always guys who survive and you're one.

SAMMY: You paying me compliments or should I get angry? (*Silence. YUSUF continues to chop vegetables and SAMMY stacks dishes.*)

YUSUF: You know what I see for the next fifty years?

SAMMY: Another prophet! Do we need more?

YUSUF: You Christians got it right. It's the end of the world. Death, death and more death. (*Beat.*) Shit. That's fatalistic crap. That's the Arab disease. Fatalism. The problem is quite simple. You me, all of us. We became the Jews of the Jews.
(*SERGE, VARDA, GIDEON, LEE and YAEL enter. YUSUF watches and works, though the family hardly notice him apart from YAEL.*)

SERGE: My wife Varda, her son Gideon Kaufmann. And her daughter Lee.

SAMMY: Lee. Like a Hollywood film star.
(*Takes jackets from them.*)

LEE: It's really Liora.

SAMMY: Lee-or-a. Gorgeous

SERGE: And this is Yael. Gideon's wife.

SAMMY: (*To SERGE.*) Oh my beautiful one. Happy Birthday. Am I allowed to kiss her?

SERGE: See I was right.

VARDA: What right?

SERGE: Private joke. Sorry about that. (*Beat.*) And he tells me the place is full, just to wind me up.

SAMMY: A very happy birthday Yael. Can I call you Yael? (*To GIDEON.*) You have very good taste.

GIDEON: (*Shaking his hand.*) I proposed to Yael here.

YAEL: A sentimental journey. We've not been here in seven years. I was twenty-three. Imagine.

SAMMY: I remember now. (*Seating everyone.*) It was champagne all round. Let me see if I have any. In the meantime there's vodka, wine.

SERGE: Wine.

SAMMY: Beer, juice. What about some starters? Hummus, aubergine. Aubergines with yoghurt, aubergines without yoghurt, with tomato without tomato, with garlic, without garlic.

SERGE: Everything. Everything. We're starving.

SAMMY: Yusuf get some of the salads ready.

VARDA: You think we're safe?

SERGE: Stop worrying.

YAEL: (*To VARDA.*) It's really good here. See you were nervy for nothing. (*She notices YUSUF.*)

VARDA: I don't know if I locked the door properly. Did you see me lock it?

SAMMY: Let's start with hummus and felafal all round then later you can decide what you want.

VARDA: If Israel ceases to exist, God forbid, you think the Danes will take us in?

GIDEON: Stop that.

LEE: Why the Danes?

VARDA: In the last war, they were the only ones to behave decently. The king and his court. They all wore yellow stars.

LEE: Hans Christian Andersen.

VARDA: You mean it's not true?

SERGE: Eat Varda. Have a drink. To Yael's birthday.

YAEL: Thanks. (*Beat.*) You know the secret of a happy marriage? One. It is important to find a man that cooks and cleans. Two. It is important to find a man that makes good money. Three. It is important to find a man that likes to have sex. Four. It is important that these three men never meet.

VARDA: Or Bulgaria. They didn't send the Jews away.

LEE: It's Yael's birthday, mother.

VARDA: I am four years older than Israel. Fifty-eight. Imagine. And now I am completely grey. I have to dye my hair. It'll give me a cancer.

LEE: Why tell everyone?

YAEL: She's right. You look so young.

VARDA: If I was thirty today then I'd be young. You don't know you're born. (*To LEE.*) And you were upside down. The doctors had to turn you.

LEE: We are eating.

SERGE: L'chaim everyone.

VARDA: And we are all acting. Acting as if there is tomorrow. Acting as if there can be peace.

SERGE: Man makes plans. God laughs.

VARDA: First the Christians want to kill us all, now the Muslims want to kill us all. What are we to do? Commit mass suicide?

SAMMY: We Christians don't want to kill you. Relax. (*Beat.*) How's business?

VARDA: What?

SAMMY: Property isn't it?

GIDEON: Oh my mother's business is fine. Isn't that right?

SERGE: Gideon.

VARDA: If you're going to be like that you might as well go back to smoking. At least when you smoked you were a bit more pleasant to be with.

GIDEON: Those apartments you buy and sell.

VARDA: What?

GIDEON: Where does all the money go?

VARDA: What's wrong with you both today? First your sister and now you?

SERGE: That's enough.

GIDEON: Is it?

SERGE: I said enough.

GIDEON: Why does nobody ask real questions in our family?

VARDA: I don't understand you. I never have.

GIDEON: You can't need the money. The apartment is paid for. All that buying and selling. War. No war.

VARDA: It's what I do.

GIDEON: Who lived there?

VARDA: What?

GIDEON: Who lived there?

VARDA: What are you talking about?

GIDEON: Before. Who lived there?

YAEL: Gideon. Leave it.

GIDEON: You never think about that?

VARDA: What are you saying? Huh? You have to start this now don't you. In public.

GIDEON: What do we have that's not public? The whole world knows everything about us and she talks about in public.

VARDA: We risk our lives to get here. Aren't we supposed to be in a restaurant celebrating?

YAEL: Gideon. It's my birthday.

LEE: He has the right to ask.

VARDA: Does he? Does he now?

LEE: Yes.

VARDA: Suddenly everybody has rights. And what about obligations?

SERGE: We lived several families in one apartment. It was always hot. Central heating courtesy of the state. Under the Communists at least everyone had a job. Now what do we have? The mafia.

GIDEON: It never crossed your mind in all the years you worked in real estate?

SERGE: What's false estate?

YAEL: Please stop this.

SERGE: Maybe it was better under the Communists.

VARDA: Crossed my mind? Crossed my mind?

GIDEON: Who lived here before May 1948?

(*YUSUF looks up.*)

VARDA: I never deal with Arab property.

GIDEON: How do you know?

VARDA: Of course I know. You think I don't know. Is that it?

GIDEON: The deeds. Do you look?

VARDA: Deeds. What are you talking about?

YAEL: Stop now.

SERGE: Are they good deeds? Sorry about that.

VARDA: No you want to talk about this, go ahead let's talk. Let the whole world hear.

GIDEON: The original owners. Who were they?

VARDA: You want to talk about the original owners? Which ones? The Romans? The Crusaders? The Ottomans? The British?

GIDEON: The Arabs.

VARDA: They never had deeds. There were no deeds. We just took over.

GIDEON: Took over?

VARDA: You talk to me of morality. The Palestinians are selling their own children. What is it? Gaddafi and Saddam pay? Ten, fifteen thousand dollars? How much do the Saudis pay? And Arafat? The European press thinks it's wonderful to be a suicide bomber. A new career option. So good for the family. And now my own son dares suggest I am selling Arab property? On one side there's the stink of the Holocaust and on the other the stink of bombs in the street. What do you want me to do? Just tell me that. What do you want me to do? Tell me. I'll do it. You want me to kill myself; is that it?

LEE: When we were children. And we lived near Haifa. I saw an old car stop in front of our house. When they got out I saw them. Three generations, standing in front. The grandmother, she was pointing to different windows. Then I realised. Our house was once their house.

VARDA: That's not true. That's just not true. You always made things up. You are trying to hurt me.

SERGE: Gideon. Lee. Why are you upsetting your mother? Sorry about that. Sammy you got some melon for everyone?

YAEL: And some water?

SAMMY: Only one piece left.

(*LEE looks at SAMMY.*)

You want it Hollywood girl?

(*She smiles and holds out her plate for the melon.*)

VARDA: Give it to Gideon. (*She snatches the melon from LEE's plate and puts it on GIDEON's. He ignores it.*) And in Europe they talk of boycotting our food. The economy is dying and none of you care.

YAEL: (*Putting the melon back on LEE's plate.*) What is it with this family, can't you behave a bit civilised?

VARDA: 'Civilised'. 'Civilised'. She comes here and talks about 'civilised'. Gideon can't you make your wife behave?

44

GIDEON: You know something, sometimes it's shit being your son.

VARDA: What? Did you hear what he said? Did you hear that?

SERGE: 'Honour thy father and mother so thy days may be long in the land of Canaan.'

LEE: (*Dryly.*) Yeh. (*Silence.*) Where's the tahini?

SAMMY: More bread? Olives? Here are the aubergines. And for you lovely lady, what's your name again? At my age the memory, it's nothing.

YAEL: Yael.

(*YUSUF looks up.*)

SERGE: A good wife, she can cook aubergines one hundred and forty-eight different ways. Isn't that what the Arabs say?

SAMMY: Garlic. No garlic. Whatever you want.

YAEL: And you know what I want for my birthday?

GIDEON: Stop now.

YAEL: This family, my family, they should know what I want.

GIDEON: I said stop.

VARDA: You didn't buy your wife a present yet?

GIDEON: You want to tell everyone our business do you? (*Beat.*)

SAMMY: I am sure Mr Kaufmann will buy his wife a lovely gift in the very near future.

YUSUF: Excuse me interrupting.

YAEL: Yes?

YUSUF: You are Mrs Kaufmann?

YAEL: Yes.

YUSUF: (*To VARDA.*) And you are also Mrs Kaufmann?

VARDA: What?

YUSUF: Mrs Varda Kaufmann.

VARDA: Yes well I was but I married a Goldstein.

SERGE: Who never makes any gold!

VARDA: (*Beat.*) Do I know you?

YUSUF: I think my father worked for you. He worked for a family Kaufmann.

VARDA: Really?

YUSUF: Did you have a worker? An Arab worker? Mahmoud Khallil?

VARDA: Mahmoud.

YUSUF: Many years ago.

VARDA: Yes. Why?

YUSUF: In your house?

VARDA: It was a long time back.

YUSUF: When I heard your name.

VARDA: (*Suspiciously.*) Yes?

YUSUF: I thought it must be you.

VARDA: More than twenty years.

YUSUF: That's right. He talks about you still.

VARDA: Really. (*Beat.*) What's your name?

YUSUF: Yusuf.

VARDA: (*Uneasily.*) How is your father?

YUSUF: Sick.

VARDA: I am sorry.

YUSUF: Not enough food. He should see a doctor.

VARDA: I am sorry.

YUSUF: He should be retired. He still looks for work.

VARDA: I am sorry. (*Beat.*) You look a lot like him.

YUSUF: Yes. (*Silence.*)

VARDA: The first son. And there was another. Mahmoud had two sons.

SERGE: What's all this?

VARDA: Before your time.

SERGE: Who's Mahmoud?

LEE: Tell him.

VARDA: Nothing.

SERGE: I am your husband. You have to tell me.

VARDA: Have to?

SERGE: What is all this?

LEE: Mahmoud was our worker. When we lived near Haifa.

SERGE: Oh?

LEE: I played on his bed. Hello Mahmoud's son. Hello Yusuf. I'm Lee. (*She shakes his hand.*) There was a hammer.

VARDA: What?

LEE: Under the pillow.

VARDA: Why were you in his room?

46

LEE: So I asked him.

VARDA: What were you doing in his room?

LEE: For God's sake.

VARDA: You have three sisters.

YUSUF: Yes

VARDA: Are they married?

YUSUF: Yes. They have children.

VARDA: Years later. He sent me a photo of two boys and you were so tall and you had your baby brother in your arms.

YUSUF: Sharif.

VARDA: You were the one he loved best.

YUSUF: How do you know?

VARDA: I know.

YUSUF: My father spoke well of you.

VARDA: (*Uneasy.*) Did he?

LEE: And he said he had the hammer because he was frightened of us.

VARDA: What?

LEE: And I said it's us who should be frightened of you, not you who should be frightened of us.

SERGE: And exactly who was Mahmoud?

LEE: He stayed over.

SERGE: Oh?

LEE: When our father was alive. He looked after the house.

GIDEON: You were always out. You always left us alone.

VARDA: The baby. Your brother. A surprise he told me.

YUSUF: Yes.

GIDEON: Every night we looked out of the window waiting for you.

VARDA: Sharif. I asked him what it means.

YUSUF: And?

VARDA: 'Honest. Worthy of trust.'

GIDEON: Where were you?

VARDA: What?

GIDEON: We hardly saw you when we were kids.

VARDA: I was busy. I was busy. Why are you asking me this now?

LEE: Why did we have servants? Why didn't you clean our house? Like other mothers?

VARDA: Why? Why? Why?

YUSUF: My father.

VARDA: Yes?

YUSUF: Mahmoud.

VARDA: Yes.

YUSUF: It's delicate.

VARDA: What.

YUSUF: Forgive me but what was he paid?

VARDA: Paid? Paid? He was paid enough.

YUSUF: With respect, that doesn't answer my question.

VARDA: He was glad to work for us.

YUSUF: Glad?

VARDA: Very glad.

YUSUF: He had a choice? (*Beat.*) You didn't say what he was paid. (*Beat.*) How much?

VARDA: It was over twenty years ago.

YUSUF: I would like to know.

VARDA: What?

YUSUF: Did you give him sick pay?

VARDA: Sick pay?

YUSUF: His employment rights?

VARDA: Are you crazy? This whole place is crazy. My daughter, my son, my husband, everyone's gone crazy here.

YUSUF: You surely remember how much he was paid?

VARDA: My husband dealt with that.

YUSUF: I thought you were the business woman.

LEE: That's right.

YUSUF: Lee?

LEE: Yes.

YUSUF: What do you remember?

LEE: Remember?

YUSUF: Did you see your parents give my father money?

VARDA: Don't say anything.

YUSUF: And you?

GIDEON: What?

YUSUF: The big boy of the house. Gideon isn't it?

GIDEON: So?

YUSUF: Mahmoud?

GIDEON: I remember him.

YUSUF: Are you in the army?

GIDEON: Everyone's in the army.

YUSUF: Not everybody.

GIDEON: What does that mean?

(*Silence.*)

YUSUF: Gideon.

GIDEON: Yeh.

YUSUF: And Lee.

YUSUF: My father. (*Beat.*) He talked about you.

SERGE: So you see we're all family. (*Beat.*) Sorry about that.

GIDEON: You know what? Your father, I never wanted him around anyway.

YUSUF: We need money now.

VARDA: What money?

YUSUF: We have to eat. We have to live. We have nothing.

VARDA: I'm sorry.

YUSUF: You threw him out.

VARDA: What?

LEE: He stole from us.

YUSUF: What?

VARDA: Mahmoud stole jewellery.

YUSUF: Oh yes?

VARDA: A diamond ring. A ruby necklace. Some gold earrings.

YUSUF: Uh huh.

VARDA: I asked him about it.

YUSUF: Really?

VARDA: My mother's jewellery. From her mother. It was for my daughter. It was for Lee. We let him go.

YUSUF: You kicked him out.

VARDA: No.

YUSUF: Are you sure he stole? (*Silence.*) The police?

VARDA: The police?

YUSUF: You told them of course.

VARDA: No.

YUSUF: Oh?

VARDA: No.

YUSUF: Why not?

VARDA: Seven years.

YUSUF: What?

VARDA: He was with us seven years.

YUSUF: That's a long time. Seven years away from his wife, seven years away from his sons.

VARDA: He went home sometimes.

YUSUF: This theft. Did you go to the police?

VARDA: How could I?

YUSUF: They would have taken your word. Jewish word against Arab word.

VARDA: He never denied it.

LEE: He was an illegal.

YUSUF: That's why you didn't go to the police?

SERGE: What?

LEE: We weren't supposed to let him stay over.

VARDA: Everyone did.

GIDEON: Not everyone.

VARDA: All our friends.

YUSUF: What about reparations?

VARDA: What?

YUSUF: For the years of my father. For the years he wasn't properly paid. For his pension now. Say five thousand dollars.

VARDA: Reparations?

LEE: Like Daddy got from the Germans.

VARDA: Lee!

SERGE: That's a lot of money.

YUSUF: I'd say five thousand was very reasonable.

VARDA: Reasonable? I bet you can build a house in Ramallah with that much.

YUSUF: What car did you drive here? (*Looking out the window.*)

SERGE: What?

YUSUF: Mercedes?

SERGE: Funny that as a name for a car. It's Spanish for the Virgin Mary, I suppose the next Volkswagen will be called Jesus.

YUSUF: You like German cars? (*Silence.*) Must be worth twenty maybe, twenty-five thousand dollars. That's an awful lot of money.

GIDEON: Enough!

YUSUF: Oh yes?

GIDEON: Did you hear me? You can't just come up to us and ask for cash.

YUSUF: Do you know what it costs me to ask you? Don't you think I have my pride? Don't you know how this tears me in half? (*Silence.*) Mr Stepfather. You like Israel?

SERGE: Of course.

YUSUF: You can live here. All the Russians can live here. But not me. You know my father was born in Jaffa. My grandfather too.

SERGE: I am a Jew.

YUSUF: You sure?

SERGE: Yes.

YUSUF: All those Russians who want to be Jews so they can live in Israel.

SERGE: My grandfather was a rabbi.

YUSUF: And my great great grandfather was Abraham.

SERGE: I told you. Same stinking family.

VARDA: Serge!

(*YUSUF is staring at YAEL.*)

GIDEON: You are staring at my wife.

YUSUF: If that bothers you, you should keep her home.

VARDA: Like your women?

YUSUF: Exactly. Only our women aren't home any more. They have a lot of learning to do. And your little sister. She's really special.

LEE: Don't talk about me as if I'm not here.

YUSUF: Little sister, you know how to shoot?

LEE: Why do you ask?

VARDA: We built this country from nothing. What did you ever do with it?

YUSUF: (*Ironic.*) That's right we just sit round all day in cafés smoking cigarettes and drinking coffee.

VARDA: Did I say that? Did I?

YUSUF: Palestine is our country.

VARDA: There is no Palestine. You have so many countries.

YUSUF: Just one.

VARDA: And suddenly, after sixty-seven, you discover you want a nation because we have one. It's jealousy. Why didn't you go to Saudi Arabia? Dubai? Kuwait?

YUSUF: And why should I move because of Poland? Or Russia. Or wherever you belong.

VARDA: The Poles killed the Jews after Auschwitz. Or maybe you don't know that?

YUSUF: And why should I move because of Poland? Because of Germany? (*Beat.*) I tried to cross the Allenby Bridge last week.

VARDA: So?

YUSUF: And you soldier boy, you stopped me.

GIDEON: What?

YUSUF: I had to get to Jordan for a wedding.

YAEL: Wedding? Whose wedding?

YUSUF: Mine.

VARDA: So?

YUSUF: And you turned me away.

GIDEON: You crazy? I wasn't even on duty last week.

YUSUF: One of your brothers then. Someone like you.

VARDA: I don't regret one single road block if it's going to stop a bomber killing my kids.

GIDEON: I was home last week.

YUSUF: It's the same thing.

VARDA: I can't stand it. In Israel, we look after our Arabs. My own daughter works with your boys. You think I wanted that you should live in camps.

SERGE: You know what. I just read, They did some research. And they found that Jews from Russia, from everywhere, Jews and Palestinians, we have the same genes! Sorry about that. (*Beat.*) I just thought of the answer to all this.

SAMMY: You ready to order? Kebabs? Roast lamb on the
bone? Yusuf you want to help with the meat?

SERGE: Let all the Arabs convert to Jews then they can
claim the right of return. (*Silence.*)

VARDA: I think I preferred it when you were whistling.

YUSUF: She is a lovely young woman, your wife.

GIDEON: Don't fuck inside my head.

SAMMY: You're hungry. That's why you're all so irritable.
Eat, drink, you'll soon feel better.

GIDEON: Do we have to listen to all this?

VARDA: And you think I don't have these thoughts too?

YUSUF: What thoughts?

GIDEON: Don't answer him.

VARDA: You think I am blind to what's going on? You
think I like to see Palestinians suffering? I hate it like
you hate it.

GIDEON: I said don't answer him.

YUSUF: Once upon a time I believed that one man was
looking after us.

SAMMY: What man?

YUSUF: But I was wrong.

VARDA: What does that mean?

YUSUF: Now I only know a man is in charge of his own
life.

VARDA: What are you talking about?

YUSUF: My father couldn't ask you for what is his, so I am
asking for him. My father is too weak so I take charge
for him. I take charge for my mother, for my brother, for
my sisters. That's a son's duty. You owe us.

VARDA: Do I go to the government in Bucharest and say,
'you owe me. Give me reparations.' Do I go back to
Romania and ask for my grandparents' house?

SERGE: They say if you shake hands with a Romanian be
sure to count your fingers.

YUSUF: But you Jews, you got reparations.

VARDA: How far do I go back? Do you know how many
countries my family fled from? I have dead relatives in
every European country. Do I go back to the Middle

Ages and ask for Crusader reparations? I should go ask the Pope?

YUSUF: Mrs Goldstein. Do you know how we are forced to live? Do you know what it's like to live in a town that is closed? Two hours a day we can go out.

VARDA: So tell me all of you, you who say I have no right to be here Do I go back? How far back? You know sometimes we have to start fresh.

SAMMY: We could go back and back and back and end up with Adam and Eve.

YAEL: (*To SAMMY.*) You know about Adam's first wife? About Lilith? She steals men's seed.

VARDA: (*Cutting across.*) You want five thousand? Where do you think I can find that? And even if I had it, you think I'd give it to you?

SAMMY: Yusuf, the meat, time to prepare the kebabs.

(*YUSUF doesn't know whether to go to the kitchen or stay.*)

GIDEON: You don't have to do this Varda. (*To YUSUF.*) Why do you come here. Interrupt our meal? Were we bothering you? Were we?

VARDA: What do you want me to do? You, Mahmoud's son.

YUSUF: Yes? Mahmoud's son!

VARDA: You want me to open a bank account. You want me to fill it with dollars for you? Sell my apartment? Sell my business? Sell my car? Clothes on my back? For your father? For all the fathers? For all the Palestinians? Then the war will stop. Is that it?

LEE: You know something mother. Mahmoud was with us night and day. He should have been with his kids but he wasn't, he was with us. Of course we never paid him properly. We gave him money to do the jobs no Jews want to do. Give him something. Get rid of it once and for all.

(*YAEL is looking at LEE.*)

VARDA: Even if I wanted to, you think I've got that kind of cash hanging about?

LEE: Righting a wrong.

VARDA: What?

YUSUF: Your daughter sees it. She understands.

VARDA: What?

LEE: (*To VARDA.*) You should listen to Mahmoud's son. Listen to someone else for once in your life. (*YAEL watches.*)

VARDA: You bitch. Don't you dare tell me what to do. (*She hits LEE. Silence. LEE walks out. GIDEON follows her.*) Out. Let's all get out of this hellhole. (*VARDA leaves with SERGE.*)

SAMMY: Come on, come on. No please, the food. Don't listen to him. Come back. (*To YUSUF.*) Look what you've done, you and your lousy five thousand dollars. You say I'm only interested in money but you've just watched I don't know how much money walk out of the door. I've got to make a living too you know. How many tourists or Israelis do you think I've got knocking on my doors and I've got a wedding to pay. Five thousand dollars is that all you can think about? I've made nothing all month and you've just ruined everything.

YUSUF: The money, it's nothing to her, nothing at all. (*Silence. SAMMY deliberately breaks a plate.*)

SAMMY: Maybe if you asked for less? (*He picks up the plate and moves away.*)

YUSUF: I should bargain?

YAEL: I'm sorry.

YUSUF: What?

YAEL: I'm sorry. (*Beat.*) I'll pay.

YUSUF: What?

YAEL: For the meal. (*SAMMY looks at her and waves his hand in dismissal.*)

YUSUF: Oh. (*He thought she meant the five thousand dollars.*)

SAMMY: No. (*YAEL opens her bag and looks for her purse.*) I said no. It's not your fault.

YUSUF: I should have asked for less.

YAEL: It's shit.

YUSUF: Yeh.

YAEL: That they turned you back at the bridge. Stopped you getting married.

YUSUF: It's not your problem.

YAEL: I'm not sure.

YUSUF: Leave it. I need to think.

SAMMY: Hey, she's being decent to you.

YUSUF: Yes.

SAMMY: The beautiful birthday girl. If I had a wife like you I'd never leave you alone for a second.

YUSUF: (*Takes the plates off the table.*) Happy Birthday.

YAEL: You hate me. It's normal.

SAMMY: Nobody could hate you. You're gorgeous.

YUSUF: I don't hate you.

YAEL: I'm a Jew.

YUSUF: I don't hate all Jews.

YAEL: My mother came from Algeria.

YUSUF: Oh?

YAEL: At home we speak Arabic.

(*YUSUF stops working and really looks at her.*)

YUSUF: You got an idea about all this?

YAEL: Your fiancée.

YUSUF: Yes.

YAEL: Do you love her?

YUSUF: Love is for fairytales. (*Beat.*) Karima.

YAEL: Is that her name?

YUSUF: Karima.

YAEL: A lovely name.

YUSUF: Your name?

YAEL: Yael?

YUSUF: What does it mean?

YAEL: Gazelle. (*Beat.*) I feel embarassed.

YUSUF: Embarassed.

YAEL: What they said to you.

YUSUF: Oh.

YAEL: I'm a stranger in this family.

YUSUF: Oh?

YAEL: This family of Europeans.

YUSUF: All this shit.

YAEL: Why do you want the money?

YUSUF: For my father. For my brother.

YAEL: Not for Karima?

YUSUF: No.

YAEL: Did you love her?

YUSUF: Love? I didn't arrive. I dishonoured her family. I dishonoured my parents.

YAEL: But it wasn't your fault

YUSUF: No. (*Beat.*) You love him?

YAEL: Who?

YUSUF: Your husband? (*Beat.*) I was jealous of Gideon and Lee. They saw our father. He was hardly home.

YAEL: What will happen to your fiancée?

YUSUF: They will arrange her another marriage.

YAEL: My grandparents' marriage was arranged. In Algiers. It lasted sixty years. (*Beat.*) Are you sad?

YUSUF: I wanted a son with Karima. I wanted to be with him the way my father wasn't with me. With us.
(*YAEL reacts. Silence.*)
Do you have a son?

YAEL: Can I have some water?

YUSUF: I am sorry. I upset you. I am indiscreet.

YAEL: I have a daughter. She's four. Michaela.

YUSUF: Oh.

YAEL: I wanted to try for a second baby. I want a boy. My husband. Gideon. He doesn't want. (*Beat.*) Why am I telling you all this? I feel I am…

YUSUF: What?

YAEL: Disloyal.

YUSUF: I like that you tell me. (*They look at one another. There is a strong charge between them. Silence.*)

YAEL: I'll get you the money.

YUSUF: What?

YAEL: I'll find a way.

YUSUF: You don't need all this.

YAEL: It's alright. I'm alright. For the first time in my life I'm alright!

YUSUF: What do you mean?
(*During this speech she talks with great passion and it attracts YUSUF.*)

YAEL: Hell it's my thirtieth birthday. I am an adult. I'm not a little girl. I don't have to answer to anyone. Only me. Lee teaches Arab kids, what do I do, I do nothing.

YUSUF: What are you talking about?

YAEL: All my life I've done what people wanted. And you know what. I'm sick of it. Sick to here with it.

YUSUF: No.

YAEL: I could get it from my mother. She always has cash in the house. Not much maybe. But I can try.

YUSUF: No.

YAEL: I could get it from my mother. She alwyas has cash in the house. Not much. But I can try.

YUSUF: No.

YAEL: Why not?

YUSUF: Not from you.

YAEL: Why not.

YUSUF: I can't explain. It's not right. That's all.

YAEL: I have to go to my mother. To pick up Michaela. I can ask her. I will call you. Before seven.

YUSUF: Do you know what you are doing?

YAEL: Yes it's crazy but I want to do something to help. Here. (*She takes off a ring.*)

YUSUF: What's that.

YAEL: My mother gave it me.

YUSUF: Why?

YAEL: When I got married. It was her mother's. It comes from Algiers.

YUSUF: It's gold.

YAEL: I don't know what it's worth. But it's worth something. You can sell it.

YUSUF: What would your mother say?

YAEL: I'll say I lost it.

YUSUF: No.

YAEL: You need money.

YUSUF: Please.

YAEL: Please.

YUSUF: Don't insult me. (*Beat.*) Yael.

YAEL: Yes.

YUSUF: That's your name. Y-a-e-l.

YAEL: Yes Yusuf.

YUSUF: No. (*Giving it back to her.*) They'll say I stole it. They'll pick me up and say I stole it from you. Like with my father.

YAEL: You don't trust me (*YUSUF shrugs. Puts it in his hand and closes it.*) Please. Take it. I want you to take it. I want you to sell it and give the money to your father. Tell him it is from a crazy Israeli woman he never met and who wishes him well. And I promise we'll never tell a soul. It will make me very happy. Will you do it? (*GIDEON enters. YAEL feels GIDEON's presence. She looks at YUSUF and at GIDEON and stands up.*)

End of Act One.

ACT TWO

Scene 4
16:00 hours

Inside the restaurant. SAMMY is peeling potatoes. YUSUF is wiping dishes. The phone rings. SAMMY replies.

SAMMY: Yes. Yes. He's here. You want him now? (*Passing the phone.*) It's for you.

YUSUF: For me? (*Takes receiver.*) Yes? Oh it's you. It's okay. I understand. What? When? Yes, I will be here. I'll be waiting. No don't tell me where it comes from. Bye. Oh and thanks.

SAMMY: Lucky you.

YUSUF: Why?

SAMMY: She calls you. I wish she calls me.

(*SHARIF enters.*)

YUSUF: Where have you been?

SHARIF: You said before five. It's four.

YUSUF: You didn't answer me.

SHARIF: And where have you been? Did the Jews come? Did you all have a lovely dinner together?

YUSUF: I've something to tell you.

SHARIF: Really?

YUSUF: Good news.

SHARIF: Good news stopped when the Jews came here.

YUSUF: I am getting money.

SHARIF: What?

YUSUF: To get you out.

SHARIF: Out?

YUSUF: Out of Jerusalem. Out of this country. Out of trouble.

SHARIF: That's the good news?

YUSUF: It'll be wonderful.

SHARIF: Will it?

YUSUF: We won't tell anyone. We'll just go. A new life.

SHARIF: A new life?

YUSUF: America.

SAMMY: Chicago is really beautiful. You ever see Chicago?

SHARIF: No.

SAMMY: You'll love Chicago. Frank Lloyd Wright. That man was really something.

SHARIF: Are you crazy? They lock up Arabs in America.

YUSUF: Okay then Canada.

SAMMY: Shi-cah-go. Magic. That skyline it's unbelievable.

SHARIF: Oh yes. Canada. You see me in Canada do you? Is that climbing the Rockies or as a mounted policeman? Maybe I could go bear hunting in the mountains. Can you believe it!

YUSUF: They aren't touching us in Canada.

SAMMY: The biggest migration of Christian Arabs, you know where it is?

YUSUF: I want you out.

SAMMY: Chile.

YUSUF: What?

SAMMY: There are so many of us in South America we could start a Christian Arab state out there!

SHARIF: Aren't there lots of Jews in Canada?

SAMMY: But they're not Israelis.

YUSUF: You could go to college next week.

SHARIF: Is that Harvard or Princeton?

YUSUF: The cash is guaranteed?

SHARIF: How? You selling dollars and euros in Ramallah or used cars in Gaza?

YUSUF: Go home now. Pack.

SHARIF: I'm not getting on any planes.

YUSUF: I want to keep you alive. For our father's sake.

SHARIF: (*Beat.*) Why did he work for the Israelis?

YUSUF: What?

SHARIF: Our wonderful father. He helped build the settlements.

YUSUF: He had no choice he would have starved.

SHARIF: Our own father.

YUSUF: Six months on Ariel. It was nothing. He got sick.

SHARIF: Well I am not going to be one of those Arabs.

YUSUF: All I ask is you come with me. Start again.

SHARIF: (*To SAMMY.*) And you too.

SAMMY: What? You too?

SHARIF: You're their servant. Doesn't it stick in your throat?

SAMMY: What?

SHARIF: Everyone in this town served the guys in charge.

SAMMY: Look when you are born here you work for whoever is boss. When I was a kid they told me this was the gateway for kings, for emperors. The Romans. The Christians. The British. (*Beat.*) They come. They go. But we stay. So what can you do? You try to lead a good life. Not to cheat, not to lie, you bring up your children well, you find them a good husband, a good wife, you hope to live long enough to have grandchildren and you die in the place your ancestors died. You try to die old. That's the best you can do. You look forward to getting wrinkles, getting bald, putting on weight. It means you lived a long life. In this place that's something. It means you survived. And then, when you go to paradise or the other place, they say a mass or a prayer for you. You hope there are a lot of people to see you off. To say you were a good person. To cry because you leave a hole where there was once a man.

(*In the distance we hear the afternoon call to prayer.*)

SHARIF: Talk. Talk. Talk. You talk to everybody. To us. To them. Who knows what you say?

SAMMY: Watch it kid. Talk like that makes people die.

SHARIF: It's you who'll do the dying not me. Your Jesus Christ. Didn't he talk danger?

SAMMY: He talked peace. Love thy enemy.

SHARIF: Well you certainly do that. (*Beat.*) Your father. What did he do?

SAMMY: He worked for the British.

(*SHARIF snorts.*)

And what do you suggest? Throwing stones or becoming suicide bombers?

SHARIF: Not suicide bombers. Those guys are holy martyrs. You Christians. You got saints too.

SAMMY: Sure we got saints. We've got lots of dead saints. The whole world is peopled with our dead saints. Your brother's right. You should travel. Visit some of our saints. Get out of here while you got the chance. Go to America. Go to France. Go to Germany. You know less than a hundred years ago, the French and the Germans were ripping each other apart. Now look at them.

(*He leaves.*)

SHARIF: I've a better idea.

YUSUF: What?

SHARIF: They want you with us.

YUSUF: They? Who's they?

SHARIF: Never mind. I told them about our conversation. They say you are a good guy. They say you are better with us than on the outside.

YUSUF: Are you crazy?

SHARIF: You want to be with me? You want to be sure I am safe? So be with me. And if you get some money then we can use that too.

YUSUF: Did you hear nothing I said? That way we'll both be killed.

SAMMY: (*From the kitchen and coming in.*) Is that table cleared?

SHARIF: The problem is I love it here.

SAMMY: You should listen to your brother.

SHARIF: You and your wrinkles and your long life, Remi never even grew old enough to grow a beard. This is the end of the world only now your Jesus Christ's not coming to save you. The end of the world and all the liars and all the murderers and all the Jews will go to hell. (*Silence.*) I never told you. (*Beat.*) I already went to another country.

SAMMY: Where?

SHARIF: I took a bus to the moon.

YUSUF: The moon?

SHARIF: It was called Tel Aviv.

SAMMY: The moon!

SHARIF: I was maybe thirteen. There were tall buildings. Lots of shops and lights. And Jews. Girls and women, with nothing on their heads, their legs, their breasts. Laughing and moving their bodies like in the movies.

SAMMY: That's beautiful!

SHARIF: And I watched them walking hand in hand with boys. Kissing in the street. They were young buying jeans, computers, all sorts of gadgets.

SAMMY: Really beautiful!

SHARIF: I saw people in restaurants. I walked into hotels with huge lobbies and a guy playing piano while people sat around drinking whisky. There were shopping malls. Concrete. Steel. Glass. Offices and theatres. Cinemas. Fucking smart cars. And it woke me up. You know that. It really woke me up.

SAMMY: That's the life we all want. What's wrong with that?

YUSUF: Tomorrow at eight, we're out of here.

SHARIF: Tomorrow at eight come to us. With the money.

YUSUF: Why do you do this to me?

SHARIF: Two more Arabs out the country. They'll be laughing. Are you with them or with us?

YUSUF: They are not all like that.

SHARIF: If they don't want to die let them get out. Why should we? (*Beat.*) You know what I want? I want to take our mother and father to Ariel. I want to settle them in one of those cool houses with air conditioning and a smart kitchen, with lots of rooms and a swimming pool and doctors and nurses and everything. That's what I want. Our father helped build Ariel. Let him live there.

YUSUF: You kill me. You turn my whole head around. I love you when you talk like that.

SHARIF: And you think I don't hurt when you say they set my place at table?

YUSUF: When you were born, upstairs. I was downstairs with him. Our mother was old to have another baby. We were worried. We thought she might die. We thought you might die. And when they told him all was well and that he had a second son. He smiled. He kissed me. And then he did something strange. He just turned on the radio and began dancing. Alone in the kitchen like that. Without going to see our mother. Without going to see his baby son. For a long time. Alone. Just dancing. And I just watched a man dance with joy because he has a new son.

SHARIF: (*Touched.*) Yes.

YUSUF: That girl.

SHARIF: What?

YUSUF: Yael.

SHARIF: What Yael?

SAMMY: Good looking. She was the daughter in law. The family your father worked for.

SHARIF: What about her?

YUSUF: She was here. They were here. The Kaufmanns. Father talked about them. Don't you remember? He worked for them. Before you were born.

SHARIF: So what.

SAMMY: They came here. To eat. Then they left.

YUSUF: But she stayed on. Wanted to help. She is going to find money for us. For you.

SHARIF: So that's it. That's what's behind all this. You got the hots for her. Some sentimental Jew. You want to fuck an Israeli girl. I might have known. We need men with balls not boys who think with their pricks.

YUSUF: That's enough.

SHARIF: Are you coming? Or do I tell them you are too much of a coward?

YUSUF: That's enough! Go home. I'll come and find you in the morning.

SAMMY: She was the real thing. She was going to find money. I heard her say so. If you'd been here. If you'd seen her. You would have felt the same way.

SHARIF: You know what. With all these Israeli girls who want to kiss Arab ass, it's too late. Far too late. You want me to meet you and get on a plane. Well I've got other plans.

(*Dog barks in the distance.*)

YUSUF: What plans?

SHARIF: I know what I have to do.

YUSUF: What you have to do? You have to go with me tomorrow to the airport because if you don't you'll never know what hit you. You'll be there waiting for me or I swear I'll kill you with my own hands.

Scene 5
Gideon and Yael's Appartment
17:00 hours

GIDEON: I walk in and you're talking like lovers.

YAEL: I was paying the bill or did nobody think of that?

GIDEON: We were sitting in the car.

YAEL: Okay.

GIDEON: Waiting.

YAEL: Yes?

GIDEON: While you.

YAEL: I told you I was paying the bill.

GIDEON: You were talking to him.

YAEL: I'm telling you the truth. What's the problem?

GIDEON: What did you say to him?

YAEL: What did I say? Nothing much. I listened.

GIDEON: And what did he say?

YAEL: Is this how you interrogate the Arabs?

GIDEON: I am going out.

YAEL: Don't run away. Everyone runs away in your family. Talk it through.

GIDEON: I want to know what was said?

YAEL: Do I have to report everything to you, like an Arab wife? (*Silence.*) Do you tell me everything? Do you hell.

GIDEON: How do I know what you were up to with him?

YAEL: Don't be ridiculous. Gideon. He was part of your life.

GIDEON: Part of my life. I never saw him before.

YAEL: You knew his father.

GIDEON: Did I ask him to work for us. Did I? I was a kid He's nothing to me. He just happens to be Mahmoud's son. End of story.

YAEL: Not end of story.

GIDEON: All this shit. Did I ask for it? Did I have any say? Our parents had an Arab stay over for seven years to do the dirty work. You think I wanted that?

YAEL: One good act.

LEE: What?

YAEL: That's all it takes.

GIDEON: God are you naive.

YAEL: One good act we could do. One small thing to help make one family live a bit better. Couldn't we do that? Your sister. She works with Jewish and Arab kids. I admire her.

GIDEON: We were waiting for you in the car. Fifteen minutes. Anything could have happened to us out in that bandit country. Didn't you think about that. Didn't you think about your own family instead of worrying about Mahmoud's? Where do your loyalties lie? With the Arabs or with us? (*Silence.*) Tell me what happened. Back there.

YAEL: I was alone with Yusuf. Talking. Why does that wind you up?

GIDEON: Because you forgot us.

YAEL: You are right. I did forget you. I thought of the young Arab and his problems and what it cost him to come up to us.

GIDEON: Cost him?

YAEL: Yes.

GIDEON: It cost him nothing. He wanted that it cost us.

YAEL: What's this really all about?

GIDEON: I can smell that kind of stuff. You think I can't smell it.

YAEL: What stuff?

GIDEON: You and him. Alone. So close.

YAEL: You make me sick.

GIDEON: From between his legs to yours. (*Silence.*)

YAEL: I don't believe what you said. I really don't believe it.

GIDEON: Who else have you had?

YAEL: What?

GIDEON: After me. Before me.

YAEL: What?

GIDEON: Who?

YAEL: Who what?

GIDEON: Men.

YAEL: What men?

GIDEON: Tell me.

YAEL: I don't believe this.

GIDEON: I need to know.

YAEL: Why this? Now? What changed?

GIDEON: Him.

YAEL: Who for God's sake?

GIDEON: Mahmoud's son.

YAEL: Yusuf?

GIDEON: Yeh.

YAEL: You can't say his name?

GIDEON: Yusuf.

YAEL: You didn't want to say it. Yusuf. Joseph.

GIDEON: I don't care for his name in this room. (*Beat.*)
Weren't you in Austria or was it Germany?

YAEL: Now what. You know I was in Heidelberg.

GIDEON: Why? Why did you go to there?

YAEL: To learn the language.

GIDEON: Not enough German Jews here to teach you?

YAEL: For God's sake.

GIDEON: Well?

YAEL: What?

(*Children's voices in the street.*)

GIDEON: So who was the German?

YAEL: What German?

GIDEON: You must have tried a German?

YAEL: Tried a German?

GIDEON: Yeh.

YAEL: Ulli.

GIDEON: Ulli? Is that Ullrich?

YAEL: Yes.

GIDEON: Tell me about Ullrich.

YAEL: He was older than me.

GIDEON: How much?

YAEL: Ten years, I can't remember, maybe twelve.

GIDEON: Good looking?

YAEL: Gideon don't fuck inside my head.

GIDEON: Ullrich. What was it with Ullrich?

YAEL: He was a mensch.

GIDEON: Really.

YAEL: He spoke about the past.

GIDEON: What past?

YAEL: His father.

GIDEON: And?

YAEL: That the old man was part of the euthanasia programme.

GIDEON: Oh?

YAEL: A Nazi doctor.

GIDEON: Mm.

YAEL: (*Not lyrically.*) It was a hot summer and in the sunshine, in the Hauptstrasse, it looked like the Middle Ages except for all the American and Japanese tourists. There were golden Catholic Marys everywhere. I had never seen that before. Mary and baby Jesus looking down on us. And all the time we were walking, he was talking about how his father was part of the burning of the books, was part of killing all those Germans, the sick and old ones who were sent to the hospitals and were murdered there. He was telling me his father was a murderer and you know I liked that he told me. Before I talked to Ulli I only met Germans who were embarassed when I said I was an Israeli, when I said I was a Jew. (*Beat.*) That day, when he spoke about his father and that he was a state murderer, it was hot but, when he told me, I got cold. (*Beat.*) And then he said, you know Yael, he's my father, and I'm supposed to love him and all I can think of is how I'm waiting for the old bastard to die.

GIDEON: Did you love him?

YAEL: What?

GIDEON: This Ulli.

YAEL: I loved the talking.

GIDEON: The talking?

YAEL: It's sexy.

GIDEON: Not bed?

YAEL: Please.

GIDEON: What was it like in bed?

YAEL: What?

GIDEON: With a German?

YAEL: I don't believe this.

GIDEON: What's it like uncircumcised?

YAEL: It's a long time ago.

GIDEON: Better than with me?

YAEL: He was circumcised actually.

GIDEON: Oh?

YAEL: Couldn't pee as a kid. They did it in the hospital.

GIDEON: Must have been nice for you then.

YAEL: Stop this.

GIDEON: So he was crap in bed and it was the talking that excited you? (*Silence.*) And in France?

YAEL: France now.

GIDEON: How old were you?

YAEL: Before the army. Seventeen. I knew a guy called Pavel. He was Czech.

GIDEON: Did he touch you?

YAEL: What?

GIDEON: Did he touch you?

YAEL: We kissed a bit.

GIDEON: Not the Czech. The Arab.

YAEL: What Arab?

GIDEON: Today.

YAEL: Yusuf. You talking about Yusuf?

GIDEON: Did he touch you?

YAEL: Why should he touch me?

70

GIDEON: You were alone with him.

YAEL: Inside the restaurant you think he touched me is that what this is all about?

GIDEON: You were alone with him.

(*Sound of cars passing and honking their horns.*)

YAEL: You want to put me in purdah.

GIDEON: What are you talking about?

YAEL: Why all these questions? Why now? (*She looks at her watch.*)

GIDEON: Have you got a date with him?

YAEL: What?

GIDEON: Why did you look at your watch?

YAEL: I thought it stopped. We have to pick up Michaela. My mother will be worried.

GIDEON: Did he touch you?

YAEL: No the Arab didn't touch me. Mahmoud's son didn't touch me. Yusuf didn't touch me. You heard me. You heard me? (*She hits out at him.*) And the women before me that you never want to talk about? (*Beat.*) Oh. I see, I am to tell you and you tell me nothing. (*Beat.*) Why don't you want a son? (*Silence.*) You never talk, you never let me go deep. Even when you look me in the eye, inside you're looking away.

GIDEON: What's that supposed to mean?

YAEL: After seven years of silence you ask me about my past but what about yours? (*Beat.*) Let's talk army.

GIDEON: Army?

YAEL: Lebanon.

GIDEON: What about it?

YAEL: You never mention it.

GIDEON: That was twenty years ago. There's nothing to say.

YAEL: Don't lie to me. (*Beat.*) You have to.

GIDEON: I have to nothing.

YAEL: This is our marriage. You want a real marriage with me Gideon or you just want to play house?

GIDEON: I can't.

YAEL: You can't what? You can't talk to me. I am your wife. Or am I just the woman you fuck?

GIDEON: Don't say that.

YAEL: Why not? It's the truth.

GIDEON: I need a drink.

YAEL: Without a fucking drink you'll tell me or I walk out of here. Out of this marriage. With Michaela.

GIDEON: I was at school with this guy.

YAEL: What guy?

GIDEON: Avi.

YAEL: Avi who.

GIDEON: Brenner. Knew him all his life.

YAEL: Go on.

GIDEON: His mother was dying of cancer when he was twelve. We sat in the schoolyard, the sun on my back when he told me.

YAEL: Yes?

GIDEON: Never cried. Never showed anything.

YAEL: Yes?

GIDEON: School. High school. Army. We went on double dates. He was like a brother. We were eighteen. What did we know?

YAEL: What did he look like?

GIDEON: Small. And funny. And square.

YAEL: Lebanon.

GIDEON: Tank regiment.

YAEL: Yes.

GIDEON: He didn't want to go to Lebanon. It was the summer. He didn't want to leave Jerusalem.

YAEL: What happened?

GIDEON: I went ahead in the jeep. Looking out to see all was clear.

YAEL: And?

GIDEON: When I came back.

YAEL: Yes?

GIDEON: His wife Dafna, she was going to have a boy. They already knew.

YAEL: And the child?

GIDEON: Yes.

YAEL: Was it a boy?

GIDEON: I need a cigarette.

YAEL: No.

YAEL: The baby?

GIDEON: Yeh.

YAEL: I need to know.

GIDEON: We had a promise. If either of us got killed and if either of us had a son, then mine would be Avi and his would be Gideon.

(*Sound of jeeps passing.*)

YAEL: And?

GIDEON: Avi.

YAEL: Avi what?

GIDEON: He was going to be a singer. In the US of A.

YAEL: What happened?

GIDEON: I went up ahead in the jeep. Those were my orders. (*Beat.*) He liked the Platters. He was kind of old fashioned for eighteen. It wasn't Beatles or Rolling Stones, no it was the Platters. He played the harmonica. For hours. Just him playing and me listening. He knew about jazz and Black music. He was terrific. He had this grandfather who lived in his house. The old boy spoke Yiddish and we used to laugh about that. He couldn't speak a word of Hebrew so Avi talked to him in Yiddish and to me it always sounded like German but sweeter. (*Laughs.*) The old man used to smell his watch, well that's what it looked like, he wouldn't wear glasses so he put his nose against it. (*Beat.*) We went out a lot on double dates and you know now I don't remember the girls I just remember how we were together. He got this heavy beard growth, and I used to watch his skin get darker during the day. Sometimes he would remember to shave before a date, twice a day he had to shave and then sometimes he would forget and when we were with the girls talking I would be staring at the man's beard growing on this kid's face.

YAEL: What happened?

GIDEON: I went up ahead. (*Pause.*) And when I got back.

YAEL: Yes. (*Silence.*) Did he die? (*Silence.*) Gideon. (*Pause.*) You've got to tell me. What happened?

73

GIDEON: He wanted to refuse. There were refuseniks back then. Did you know that?

YAEL: No.

GIDEON: He wanted to refuse but he also wanted to do his duty. To his family. Why didn't he just leave? If he'd left, he'd be here now.

YAEL: What happened to Avi?

GIDEON: Did I tell you he played the mouth organ?

YAEL: Yes.

GIDEON: I found it.

YAEL: Where?

GIDEON: All burnt too.

YAEL: Hizbollah?

GIDEON: All of them.

YAEL: So that's it.

GIDEON: Yes.

YAEL: How?

GIDEON: While I was up ahead with the other guys, in the jeep.

YAEL: Yes?

GIDEON: Yes.

YAEL: Yes what?

GIDEON: Grenades.

YAEL: Where?

GIDEON: Grenades thrown into all the tanks. I couldn't save him. I should have been with him.

YAEL: Don't say that.

GIDEON: Every morning, his name in my mouth.

YAEL: Yes.

GIDEON: I went with him to his mother's funeral. We were both thirteen. He said kaddish. It broke me up.

YAEL: And the baby?

GIDEON: On the way to Lebanon, he told me, his mother, she beat him. Told me he was glad she was dead. And I'm wondering if at that moment, when he was saying kaddish, did he remember her beating him? (*Silence.*) One minute we're together and the next they are lowering him. In a sheet. Into the earth.

YAEL: The baby.

GIDEON: What?

YAEL: You heard.

GIDEON: (*Beat.*) Lost at six months. No baby Gideon.
(*Beat.*) Lee tells me she fucks around.

YAEL: Lee?

GIDEON: Not just Jake. Maybe she's out there now. On the
street. Why do you think she does that? (*Silence.*)

YAEL: There's something else.

GIDEON: What?

YAEL: There's more you haven't told me.

GIDEON: Why does she do it? I hate it. (*GIDEON throws a
boot across the room.*)

YAEL: Tell me everything. Gideon. I have to know.

GIDEON: Last December. Ramallah. The boys were
throwing stones at us. They came from everywhere. I got
out of the tank. I went up to one of the kids. I dragged
him into a field. I made him kneel. I blindfolded him. I
tied his hands behind his back. His breathing it was very
fast, he was sweating. I lifted my rifle. I didn't know what
I was going to do. I wanted to smash him to the ground.
I wanted to beat and beat until there was nothing left of
him. There was a crack and then another. Sharp. Steel
against bone. He whimpered and I heard screaming. It
was me. Just screaming at him, try throwing stones now.
(*With irony.*) 'And Gideon was a great warrior and the
people proclaimed him as their leader. And they said
you will rule us and your sons will rule us. And Gideon
said I will not rule over you, neither shall my son rule
over you: the Lord shall rule over you.' (*Laughs. Beat.*) I
never told anyone. You wanted to know. Now you've got
it. Satisfied? (*Silence.*) With you I tried to make a life.
With you there was no taste of acid in my mouth. With
you a woman was more than just a fuck. And when
Michaela was born I was glad she wasn't a boy.

YAEL: Yes.

GIDEON: His child's bone snapping. I can feel it now. His
face green with shock. He shit himself with fear. He
thought I was going to kill him. (*Beat.*) I vomited all
over my uniform. (*Silence.*) You feel better now you

know? You don't think sometimes it's best to keep your
mouth shut?

(*He sobs uncontrollably. YAEL watches.*)

YAEL: It's the first time you've really talked to me. You
know that?

GIDEON: I can't go back there. To the territories.

YAEL: Is there a choice?

GIDEON: I'll do anything but I can't go back.

(*An Alsatian barks in the distance.*)

YAEL: Okay.

(*GIDEON puts on his army jacket but buttons it up wrongly
several times.*)

GIDEON: I am banging on metal doors, I am chasing kids
who throw stones down an alley, I am tearing up
mattresses to see what's hidden inside, I am pulling
people out of their beds, I am listening to babies crying,
women screaming, I am carrying men shackled in the
back of the jeep.

YAEL: I know. I know.

GIDEON: You know nothing.

YAEL: Alright.

GIDEON: Avi wanted to refuse twenty years ago and now I
understand what he meant. He understood more at
eighteen than I do now. They'll put me in jail. I don't
care. They'll treat me like shit but I don't care. (*Beat.*)
I'll report in the morning. At eight. I'll report and I will
refuse to serve in the territories. They'll say I'm a
coward, you can live with that? Being Gideon-the-
coward's wife? (*Silence.*) I'll be maybe half a year in jail,
then they'll call me up again but I'll refuse again. (*Beat.*)
I may be a rotten Israeli but at least I can try to be a
decent Jew. (*Silence. He makes to leave with his badly-
buttoned jacket and kit bag.*)

YAEL: Where are you going? I'll come with you.

GIDEON: I have to be alone. I am going to get cigarettes.
(*Beat.*) You and him. Seeing you together. My chest hurts.
You know that?

Scene 6
Varda's office
19:00 hours

The Muslim call to prayers is heard in the distance.

VARDA: What a day. What a stinking hellish day.
SERGE: That kid.
VARDA: What?
SERGE: He upset you.
VARDA: Everything upsets me. My own children upset me.
SERGE: Why do we have them?
VARDA: You know the problem. Too much history. Not enough geography.
SERGE: What?
VARDA: That's the problem.
    (*Phone rings.*)
SERGE: Your mother.
VARDA: Switch it to message. I can't face her meschugass now.
SERGE: What was he like?
VARDA: Who?
SERGE: Mahmoud.
VARDA: Mahmoud. He was okay.
SERGE: That doesn't tell me much.
VARDA: You think the deal'll go through?
SERGE: I mean if I met him in the street I'd like to know who he is.
VARDA: You won't meet him in the street.
SERGE: Did something happen between you?
VARDA: What does that mean?
SERGE: Stupid Russian feelings. I know when you like a man. I know you.
VARDA: I used to see him dancing when I was in another room. Music from the forties.
SERGE: Yes? (*Pause.*) Varda!
VARDA: That's it.
SERGE: I knew there was something, He wanted you.
    (*Beat.*) He excited you?

VARDA: Don't be ridiculous!

SERGE: Why did you ask him to leave?

VARDA: Why? Because.

SERGE: Because what? (*Beat.*) That's all? And the jewellery?

VARDA: I don't want to talk anymore.

SERGE: Varda. I am your husband. We have to talk. About everything.

VARDA: Serguei. I'm exhausted. This day is the longest in my life.

(*Sound of children in the street and sirens in the distance mixed with the Arab call for prayer.*)

SERGE: Let's go home.

(*YAEL comes in breathless.*)

YAEL: Is Gideon here?

VARDA: Why should he be here?

SERGE: (*To YAEL.*) You want a coffee?

YAEL: He left.

VARDA: What do you mean he left?

YAEL: He walked out.

VARDA: At this time? Where would he go?

YAEL: I thought here.

(*VARDA dials his number.*)

VARDA: You had a row?

SERGE: You want sugar?

YAEL: A row?

VARDA: You had a row and he walked out. What's wrong with everyone today. He's going to the army tomorrow and you had to have a row tonight? What are you thinking of?

SERGE: Drink it while it's hot. (*Offers it to YAEL. She doesn't register.*)

VARDA: Nothing. Why does he always turn it off. I told him. Yes. Did you have a row? Can you tell me that? Yael, a wife should bring a bit of calm to the house not aggravate the situation.

YAEL: We didn't row.

VARDA: Oh?

YAEL: He's not going to the army anymore.

VARDA: What do you mean, 'he's not going to the army anymore'?

YAEL: He's become a refusenik.

VARDA: What?

YAEL: You heard.

VARDA: A refusenik. That's not possible. They'll put him in jail. His name will be mud. Nobody will give him work.

YAEL: He decided. It's definite.

VARDA: My son. A refusenik. Well maybe it's good. Maybe in jail at least he's safe. I don't know. I don't know what to say. I don't know what's right or wrong anymore.

SERGE: What's his number. I'll call him.

VARDA: Where could he be? Maybe he's with Lee.

YAEL: Maybe he just went to a café.

VARDA: A café? A café? Please God no.

YAEL: I should go home. He may be back now.

SERGE: Shall I drive you?

VARDA: Or a friend?

YAEL: He has no friends.

SERGE: Sorry about that.

VARDA: No friends. That's not possible. A boy his age.

SERGE: I'll drive you.

YAEL: Did he tell you about Lebanon?

SERGE: In five minutes you'll be home. He'll be waiting for you.

VARDA: Lebanon? What are you talking about?

YAEL: When he was in Lebanon?

SERGE: He'll be worried if he gets back and you're not there.

VARDA: That was twenty years ago.

YAEL: What did he say?

VARDA: He was a kid. The army. How do I know?

YAEL: He must have spoken about it?

VARDA: You think eighteen year old boys talk to their mother? They come home with their washing.

YAEL: What about Avi. The baby?

VARDA: Avi which Avi? Yael, what are you talking about?

YAEL: Did he speak to Lee? He must've spoken to someone.

VARDA: Spoken to someone? About what?

YAEL: Where is Lee? Maybe he's out there looking for her.

VARDA: Why should he be looking for Lee? Is she ill?
(*Beat.*) I can't believe he won't go to the army. Everyone was so proud to serve in our family. My father, my mother, Heiner. I was proud.

SERGE: 'I promise to love my motherland and defend her to my death and if I betray her let the hard hand of my peoples be my punishment.'

VARDA: What?

SERGE: It's what we swore in the army.

YAEL: I didn't know you were a soldier.

SERGE: Everyone was. If you refused they put you in the hospital and gave you injections and said you were mad. I had a friend. He was a hammer-thrower from Byelorussia, a great sportsman. When I saw him a year after they took him, he said Sergueil, let's go, drink. This man never drank, he was always looking after his body, an athlete. But they killed that in him. We bought eau de cologne and we drank it to forget.
(*Explosion in the distance. Lights flash.*)

VARDA: Oh God, are you alright. Serguei? Yael? (*She holds them to her tightly.*) Oh God, thank God we're alive, we're alive, we're all alive.
(*Lights fade. Sounds of explosion. Sirens. Mobile phones.*)

Scene 7
The Hospital
07:00 hours

The Muslim call to prayer is heard in the distance. Silence.

YAEL, VARDA and LEE are sitting in silence. They have been there most of the night. SERGE is whistling from 'Orpheus and Eurydice'.

SERGE: Anyone want a drink?

VARDA: The door. I'm not sure I locked it.

SERGE: What door?

VARDA: The car. Go and see. (*Beat.*) He's going to die. I'll kill myself.

LEE: We don't know that.

VARDA: He looks dead. Why did they send us out of the room? Why did they send us out of the room? Tell me that.

(*Her mobile phone rings.*)

SERGE: Your mother.

VARDA: I can't talk now.

SERGE: I'll put it on message. (*Silence. Looking around. He doesn't know what to say.*) Nice hospital. Sorry about that.

VARDA: Why didn't I have more children?

LEE: I'm here mother.

VARDA: I wanted more. (*Beat.*) Why are you picking your teeth?

SERGE: Something stuck. A pumpkin seed.

VARDA: Now you eat like the Arabs? Oh God. Please don't let him die. I want to believe in God. But he's a madman. He hates us all.

SERGE: Varda. I'll get you a coffee. (*There is a tray with some cups but no coffee machine or kettle.*)

VARDA: Talk to me. Tell me something. Something to stop my brain splitting through my skull.

SERGE: What can I tell you Varda? I lost a son in Kabul and you want me to talk. What can I say? We should have won in Afghanistan. We should have won. My son would still be alive. He'd be here in this room now. I am trying to think of something to say but it all comes out wrong. (*Silence.*) The first time I saw you. At that barmitzvah. You came over and asked me to play something. What was it? The Anniversary Waltz. And I looked at you and I thought, I like that woman. I thought this woman, I know it's vulgar, but I thought yes, she has balls.

(*Silence. VARDA's mobile rings. She answers.*)

VARDA: No mother we're not coming to dinner now. No mother, we're not getting on any buses. (*She turns it off.*) Why does she talk of buses now? You think she guesses?

SERGE: She has balls. That's what I thought.

VARDA: When I was fourteen I used to take buses to school. In Tel Aviv. It was before the Six Day War. There were beggars everywhere, children with broken arms and legs. The parents did it so they could beg. Can you imagine doing that? And the crowds in the bus station; I used to push myself to the front. I used to swirl between the people. I've always been able to get through crowds like that. But, when I was on the bus, I couldn't work out why all these men were pressing rolled up newspapers into my back. How could I have been so naive?

LEE: You never told me that.

VARDA: Why am I thinking of that now?

(*VARDA's phone rings.*)

Yes? What? No? Pleased of course I'm pleased. Bye.

SERGE: What?

VARDA: The loan.

SERGE: Yes.

VARDA: I've got the loan.

SERGE: Yes.

VARDA: For the whole block.

SERGE: The tree?

VARDA: It can stay.

SERGE: We should celebrate. Sorry about that.

(*SERGE starts whistling 'Orpheus and Eurydice'. VARDA wants to tell him to stop but doesn't dare.*)

YAEL: He was upset. That I was talking to Yusuf.

LEE: (*Cutting across.*) You know something? (*Beat.*) I'm not convinced Mahmoud stole the jewellery.

VARDA: What?

LEE: You said it was for me. But you never gave me a thing your whole life. If there was any jewellery at all from your mother to me, then you kept it.

VARDA: What?

LEE: Either way you deceived us all. Either you lied about Mahmoud or you stole from me.

VARDA: What?

LEE: And I don't think he was a thief.

VARDA: What?

LEE: The jewellery he was supposed to have stolen. You made it up. You were in touch after he left. It doesn't make sense if he was the thief you say he was.

VARDA: Someone took a razor and they ripped my insides.

LEE: The whole story, you made it up.

VARDA: And why would I do that?

LEE: And I believed you!

YAEL: Is it true?

VARDA: That I am a liar and a thief of course it's true. And a murderer. (*Beat.*) Alright you want to know the truth, why not. My son is dying upstairs. That's the truth. He danced for me. That's right. (*Beat.*) This young man dancing. Just for me. In my own house. And it happens. Can't be stopped. Mahmoud. His bed. His tiny room. Crazy thought. Lying in his arms. Anxious. As if I expect me to walk in on us. I tell him you have to go. I gave him the jewellery. And so when Yusuf came today, and yes, when he came to ask me for money... (*Laughs.*) So now you know. (*Silence.*) Sing something Serge. (*SERGE starts the Soviet national anthem and then stops realising what he has sung.*)

SERGE: Sorry about that. Old army habits. (*SERGE starts singing the strain from 'Orpheus and Eurydice' but he can't continue. Silence.*)

VARDA: Who was it who said this would never be a real country like all the others until we had thieves and prostitutes. (*Beat.*) Well we've got that. And we've got war. And now we are a real country they talk of the end of us. (*Laughs.*) You know this country was to make Jews safe!

LEE: Why did you lie about Mahmoud?

SERGE: Stop this Lee.

VARDA: Why did you turn so hostile? You were such a pretty little girl. In your little dresses.

LEE: You mean it's a pity I had to grow up. (*Silence. Trying not to cry.*) You know I hardly remember you when we were kids. What do I see? I see Daddy sitting at the foot of my bed singing me to sleep. Who makes breakfast for us? Who makes tea when we come home? Daddy. You were always on the phone. You know what my childhood was? It was Gideon. When we lived in Haifa and we were both going to primary school, Mahmoud used to take us to the bus. I think it was the number four. (*Beat.*) And because Gideon was older he would sit in the front with his friends and ignore me. It hurt so bad I cried all day in school.

VARDA: Lee. I have to tell you something. (*Beat.*) I may be a rotten mother. And maybe I can't show what you want me to show but whatever you say to me, however hard you try to hurt me, I love you the best I can. And maybe I loved Gideon more and that was wrong I know that but you can't choose who you love. (*LEE reacts as if she has been hit.*) It doesn't work that way. Because you have a child you don't always feel what you are supposed to feel. Maybe if you were married and had kids I'd feel better, I'd know who you are. And now he's dying and I am dying too can't you see that. I gave him life and now they are ripping it out of me. He's upstairs fighting to live and here in my guts, in my womb I have such pain you can't imagine. (*She howls in agony and sobs from deep within. Her breathing becomes fast.*) I can't feel my hands or my feet. They are dead. I can't feel the blood in my hands. (*She moves her hands. SERGE rubs her back.*)

SERGE: It's alright, you are going to be alright.

VARDA: I don't think I can walk.

SERGE: Come on. It's the shock. Try and walk. Let's see if we can find a doctor in this hospital. (*He makes her get up and she walks very tentatively.*) You see. You can walk. Come on we'll go and find something to drink. Pity there's no vodka. (*VARDA leaves with SERGE. Silence.*)

YAEL: Maybe you're too hard on her.

LEE: (*Beat.*) I'm sorry. I'm so sorry. It's a hell family and you walked right into it. I'm going outside.

YAEL: I want us to go upstairs. To see him. Together.

LEE: I can't stand to be near her.

YAEL: For him. Not for her.

LEE: You're right.

YAEL: Let's go.

LEE: I'd even be prepared to believe in God if only he'd let Gideon live. I can see him blown high into the air. Why wasn't it me?

(*She leaves to go outside but YUSUF enters. He is surprised to see YAEL and LEE.*)

YAEL: What are you doing here? Did you come for the money? I never got it.

YUSUF: And you?

LEE: Why are you here?

YUSUF: My brother.

YAEL: Yusuf. I don't have the money.

YUSUF: My brother.

LEE: What are you talking about?

YUSUF: Sharif.

YAEL: What with your brother?

YUSUF: He disappeared.

YAEL: What?

YUSUF: They found his cell phone.

YAEL: What?

YUSUF: By the bus.

YAEL: Why are you here? What do you want? I haven't got the money.

YUSUF: My brother.

LEE: You are here to see your brother?

YUSUF: Yes. They told me to come. To identify him. Now I have to answer questions.

YAEL: He's dead? How? (*Beat. Letting go of her emotion for the first time.*) I heard the explosion. It was just near the bus station. I heard the sirens and the screams and I began running. The bus was on its side all burnt out and people were howling. I had to get him away. Children talking and laughing and an explosion and I was running and running and he was furious. There were others I didn't tell him about. You think that's bad? Once I tried to count how many. Then when I was walking down the street, I'd remember another guy.

YUSUF: I want you to listen.

YAEL: At the top of the Hauptstrasse near the Schloss, in this bar, there are these photos of students. They have duelling scars. To prove they are men.

YUSUF: Yael. Listen to me.

YAEL: All this dying. Every day. And I think you've got to live now, every minute of every day. Now! Now! Now!

YUSUF: Sharif.

YAEL: Don't fuck inside my head. (*Laughs.*) I even talk like him.

YUSUF: The money. It was for New York.

LEE: Why does everyone want to go to New York?

YAEL: Shouldn't you be married? To that girl. Oh I forgot, they stopped you.

YUSUF: My brother.

YAEL: I never had a brother. We were all girls. They told me, 'Run away and get married we can't pay a dowry.' (*Beat.*) I wanted a brother. For Michaela.

LEE: Your brother on the bus? Is that what you're saying?

YUSUF: What am I going to do now?

LEE: How could your brother be on the same bus? What was he doing there?

YUSUF: I don't know. I don't know. The bus was going to Akko. Why would he go to Akko? I told him go home not to the north.

LEE: Yes, that's right. There were Arab kids in the bus. You kill your own too you know that?

YAEL: And I trusted you? And I was giving you my ring? And I was looking for money for you? (*YAEL gets up and hits YUSUF as hard as she can.*) You betrayed me.

LEE: Did your brother try to kill my brother? Is that what you're telling me?

YUSUF: Burnt alive. There was a ring. My father gave it him. That's how I knew.

YAEL: What ring?

YUSUF: I was so scared he'd be the one who blew up the bus.

YAEL: And he didn't?

YUSUF: I should've got him out. I should've done more. It's my fault.

YAEL: I talked alone with you. And Gideon, my husband, he was so hurt. Why did I do that?

YUSUF: What do I tell my father? My mother? That I lost him? He's their baby.

YAEL: Where's my baby?

(*SERGE enters and looks at YAEL. She understands from his expression that GIDEON is dead. YAEL howls.*)

No-o-o-o-o-o-o-o! Please God. Don't do this.

(*VARDA walks in, looking blank. In the silence LEE puts an arm around her mother. SERGE absentmindedly sings the aria from 'Orpheus and Eurydice'. VARDA takes a cup and smashes it against the wall. YUSUF looks at them and slowly rips his shirt. Lights fade and the last image holds on YUSUF alone tearing his shirt.*

As he does, somewhere in the distance of the Jerusalem morning, children's voices are heard in the street. A siren moans and a clock strikes eight.)

The End

THE GOLEM

A new play for children based
on the Yiddish legend

to my aunt Edith Newman

Why I wrote The Golem

It's no accident that *The Golem* was written at one of the bloodiest moments in Israel's history. I started it in Spring 2002 at the height of the Second Intifada when the fate of Israel's existence seemed in doubt and when Jews everywhere asked themselves fundamental questions about the morality of violence.

However my Golem is not written in a Ghandiesque mood of passive resistance. Rather, it is the reflection of the eternal split in the Jewish psyche. For centuries the obligation of Jews has been to study Talmud (for men only). This devotion to learning and to God has led to the stereotype of the bookish shortsighted Jew in a long kaftan and enclosed in his own world. After the Holocaust, a new Jew emerges, a warrior inextricably linked to a state of Israel which has exiled another people, the Palestinians.

The Arabs call the 1948 setting up of the State of Israel the Catastrophe. To them, the Jews are the invading force which displaces them. Now we have these two seemingly contradictory pictures of Jews. The student, the rabbi, the moralist versus the warrior, the coloniser, the immoralist. How to come to terms with these two media images, especially after September 11 when the East / West struggle polarised into a much larger world conflict?

I have no answers to these questions; they were just the background to the writing of a simple play for children which also reflects some of the issues around self-defence, isolation, exclusion, exile and creativity. Although *The Golem* comes out a Yiddish legend, the story can fit any situation and any people. I deliberately do not use the word Jew in the text but it is clear to those with a sense of history that the people with the yellow patches are Jews.

Although the yellow star was used by Adolf Hitler to ghettoise Jews, the yellow patch in fact comes from Vatican orders when Jews where ordered into the medieval Venice Ghetto. The first prejudice against Jews was from Catholics and, it is only after the setting up of the state of Israel that

Arab antisemitism becomes apparent. Traditionally before 1948 Jews lived more easily amongst Muslims than Christians. And in India, Jews never suffered discrimination.

Last year, Adrian Berry, Director of the Bull, suggested to me that I write a Jewish play for children as there is no Jewish youth theatre in Britain at the moment. I decided to make the story a modern play as part of my own interest in writing contemporary Jewish British theatre. I also wanted to explore the theme of violence and self-defence within the framework of the original Golem story. The few words of Yiddish in the text is a homage to a disappeared world annihilated in the Nazi death camps. It is also a memory of my own Yiddish-speaking grandparents and great grandparents who came from Romania and Lithuania. We, their grandchildren, were not taught the many languages they spoke as the impulse to assimilate fast was primary. But the underlying worries about self-defence, difference and assimilation remained strong if unarticulated as we grew up.

In the dramaturgy, the figure of the grandmother is presented as a puppet. She symbolises the past we all carry with us. (She does not exist in other versions of *The Golem*.) For me, the grandmother is a motif for unfinished business. If we can't explore our own families' previous culture and / or history, it is difficult for us to get on with living and as I write this, I also think of the many Germans I have met who still have to deal with their own family history. Those of us who come from strong faith-based cultures do not have to believe in the religion stamped on us at birth but we do have to know where we come from in order to understand the many elements that make up our personality. I am a Jewish atheist and yet I have studied as much as I can about Jewish culture, Christianity and the Koran.

In this play, the grandmother cannot marry and her children and grandchildren cannot be born until her descendents learn how to defend themselves. I am playing with time zones and with the imagination to explore how the individual can learn to be strong without being destructive in her society. Each of us carries our own Golem inside and we need to know how to use its wildness creatively.

All children of immigrants know that prejudice can strike at the most unexpected moments and some internal strategy needs developing fast to minimise hurt. When I was five and in primary school, a blonde girl screamed at me in the playground, 'You killed Jesus.' Precociously I retorted, 'No I didn't, I wasn't there.' The battle lines were already drawn and perhaps, because of that moment, I write this play now.

Notes

The first production was performed with a gauze backdrop. It was inked in with shapes suggesting the city of Prague. A huge book and a tall doll on a stick were the other props. There was also an umbrella which opened up with hanging stars suspended inside. A long piece of blue silk was pulled out of the book, suggesting the sea, the river and other imagery. This was a very minimal vision and, of course, the director is free to use or discard these ideas. The aesthetic suggested the paintings of Marc Chagall and the physicality of Vsevolod Meyerhold's Theatre. Costumes were plain trousers, jackets and caps except for the rabbi who had a long black coat, a hat and white socks. Joseph Golem wore a coat-jacket with multicoloured strips as the lining.

I intended the styles to be both music-hall with the vaudeville tradition of two almost-tramp like Chaplinesque figures. In this way I wanted the play to transcend cultures but to also engage in an early twentieth century popular theatre aesthetic. The writing reflects this and there is plenty of space in the scenario for movement, music and physicality.

Kyla Greenbaum wrote an original score for this production which can be used with her agreement.

Characters

GOLDMAN

MANGOLD

RABBI

GOLEM

BRIDE
a puppet

Mangold and Goldman can be male or female actors

The Golem was first peformed first at The Bull Theatre, London on 11 September 2002, with the following cast:

THE GOLEM, Liam Smith

RABBI, Abdala Keserwani

GOLDMAN, Kris Brookman

MANGOLD, Theresa Aldridge

Director, Liselle Terret

Designer, Nicolai Hart-Hansen

Design of the Bride Puppet, Irene Wise

Lighting Design, Ian Watts

Original Music, Kyla Greenbaum

Sound Design, Colin Brown

Lights up. Music. All cast come on stage and stand at angles, staggered against one another.

GOLDMAN: A long time ago in the heart of a land called Europe lived a special group of people. These people were called the people with the yellow patches.
(*Everyone puts on a coat with yellow patches.*)

MANGOLD: But these people were not allowed to live in the centre of the town. They were forced to live in a walled area called a ghetto.
(*Music. CAST make a wall.*)

GOLDMAN: But who are these people with yellow patches? Are they the same as you and me? Do they have horns? Do they have tails?

MANGOLD: No. They are like everyone else. They get up in the morning. They eat their breakfast. They play music. They sing songs. They dance. They fall in love. They get married. They have children. Just like everyone.
(*The CAST pose for a family photo.*)

GOLDMAN: (*To audience.*) So why are they behind a wall?

MANGOLD: Because the people without the yellow patches force them to stay there.

GOLDMAN: But why?

MANGOLD: Because the people with the yellow patches have special books.
(*A cast member juggles suggesting magic and imagination.*)

GOLDMAN: And what is in these books?

MANGOLD: Everything. Music. Magic. Stories of angels coming down from the skies on a ladder. Stories of kings and prophets. Stories of planets and stars. Stories of a man called Jonah who is swallowed by a whale. Stories of a man called Noah who builds an ark to save all the people and all the animals when the world is flooded.

GOLDMAN: Stories of a dove carrying an olive branch in its beak. Stories of a man called Absalom who is riding on a horse when his hair gets trapped in a tree.

MANGOLD: Stories of when we were in Egypt and frogs and lice and boils hurt everybody else but us. Stories of how we are running away from danger and how the sea parts in the middle so that we can escape.

GOLDMAN: Stories of how great King Solomon travels all the way to Africa.

MANGOLD: A–f–r–i–c–a.

GOLDMAN: To a country called Ethiopia where there is a queen called Sheba.

MANGOLD: And he falls in love with her.

GOLDMAN: What's falling in love?

MANGOLD: You'll find out soon enough. Let's stick to the story of the people with the yellow patches, the people who love learning.

GOLDMAN: And one man in particular, a great rabbi.

MANGOLD: What is a rabbi?

GOLDMAN: A rabbi is a teacher, you nebbish.
(*Hits him playfully.*)

MANGOLD: What's a nebbish?

GOLDMAN: A fool like you.
(*Hits him again.*)

MANGOLD: Ow. You must not hit me.

GOLDMAN: And why not?

MANGOLD: Because it's not fair. I like peace, I don't like hitting.

GOLDMAN: Then don't be such a nebbish, nebbish.

MANGOLD: Tell me about the rabbi.

GOLDMAN: The rabbi loves to read everything he can find. This rabbi is tall and very clever. And one day, the people outside the wall, the people without the yellow patches on their coats, they throw stones at the people with the yellow patches. They come to fight with the men and push the people around until they are terrified.

MANGOLD: I hate fighting. I just want to stay home in peace.
(*GOLDMAN mimes defending himself from imaginary hordes while MANGOLD quakes.*)
Go away and leave us alone!

(*Knockabout fight for 5–8 year olds. More realistic fight for older children.*)

(*Looking at the doll.*) Who is that?

GOLDMAN: Can you see her too?

MANGOLD: Of course I can see her.

GOLDMAN: How strange.

MANGOLD: Why strange?

GOLDMAN: Because she is my grandmother.

MANGOLD: And why is your grandmother wearing a wedding dress? And why is she getting married?

GOLDMAN: She's not getting married, she's waiting to get married.

MANGOLD: Why? I don't understand?

GOLDMAN: Why? Why? Why so many questions?

MANGOLD: Yes why?

GOLDMAN: You like asking questions huh?

MANGOLD: Don't you?

GOLDMAN: Why do you always answer a question with another question?

MANGOLD: Why do I always answer a question with another question?

GOLDMAN: You're doing it again!

MANGOLD: You didn't answer why your grandmother is waiting to get married.

GOLDMAN: Why? Because there is too much danger.

MANGOLD: Danger?

GOLDMAN: And again!

MANGOLD: Again?

GOLDMAN: Asking questions.

MANGOLD: Am I?

GOLDMAN: Listen. She can't get married while we are being attacked. We have to wait.

MANGOLD: Wait?

GOLDMAN: That's right. She is from a different time. For her, time has stopped and she cannot get married until the danger goes away. And if she cannot get married, our parents cannot be born. Does that answer your question?

MANGOLD: Yes and no. But what about this 'different time'? I see her and you see her but she is not here?

GOLDMAN: You and I, we see things other people don't see. We can see what happened before we were born.

MANGOLD: So I am clever and I am not a nebbish afterall!

GOLDMAN: Wrong. You are still a nebbish but because I am here you see what I see.

MANGOLD: Why is your grandmother here with you now?

GOLDMAN: Because she is the wise woman and she goes with me everywhere. She watches over me.

MANGOLD: I wish I had a grandmother who did that too.

GOLDMAN: You can share mine if you want.

MANGOLD: Can I really?

GOLDMAN: Yes so let's get on with the story. Grandma is in danger and can't get married to my grandfather as there are no weddings until we are at peace.

MANGOLD: That's right so what can we do to have peace? What can we do against the people who want to hurt us rabbi?

GOLDMAN: Yes rabbi what are you going to do to save our people?

MANGOLD: You are a clever man. You know all about magic.

(*RABBI consults a large book.*)

RABBI: I could make someone to defend us.

GOLDMAN: Yes make us someone. Oh rabbi. Hurry hurry.

MANGOLD: How can you make a human being?

GOLDMAN: The rabbi can do anything. He knows what is in books and he can create something from nothing.

MANGOLD: From nothing?

RABBI: But is this wise?

(*Music suggesting his indecision.*)

MANGOLD: Do it now.

RABBI: Who knows what might happen if I magic up a new being?

MANGOLD: Just get rid of the danger rabbi so our grandmother can get married and our parents can be born.

RABBI: I don't know. I really don't know.

GOLDMAN: Go for it rabbi.

RABBI: I'm not sure.

GOLDMAN: Rabbi you must.

RABBI: Must? Must? Must I? Must I make a man? Must I make a monster? If I must then I must go to a room with no windows, a room with no doors.

GOLDMAN: A room with no windows. A room with no doors. How can that be?

RABBI: (*Tapping his head.*) In here. This is the room with no windows. The room with no doors.

GOLDMAN: Do I have a room with no windows? No doors?

RABBI: Everybody has.

GOLDMAN: So how do I go there?

RABBI: You go there every night.

GOLDMAN: Do I?

RABBI: When you sleep.

GOLDMAN: What?

RABBI: When you close your eyes you see pictures?

GOLDMAN: Yes.

RABBI: Those are the pictures in the room without walls, the room without windows. (*Beat.*) I will take clay and from this clay I will make a man. From the air, from the fire, from the water, from the earth.

GOLDMAN: And how do you mix all these to make a man?

RABBI: This is a secret which nobody must ever know. I will amaze you because I will create something which will protect us all. And this creature will be called a Golem.

MANGOLD: A Golem? That's a strange word.

RABBI: And this Golem will not eat or drink. He will not need payment.

GOLDMAN: What is a Golem? A robot?

RABBI: If you like. The Golem will work and he will never answer back. But most important of all, he will defend us.

GOLDMAN: Will he fight for us?

RABBI: The question is should I make this Golem? Should I make a fighter?

GOLDMAN: Yes, yes.

RABBI: But what if I can not control him?

MANGOLD: Stop worrying rabbi.

RABBI: He might be too strong for me.

GOLDMAN: But you have strong brains.

RABBI: What if he turns against me?

GOLDMAN: Stop worrying.

RABBI: But is it right to make a creature?

MANGOLD: You are a good man. You will make a good creature.

RABBI: We must watch him night and day. Come with me.
(*GOLDMAN and MANGOLD become his assistants. There is music and movement during the next speech.*)
Now we will go down to the river.
It is four in the morning. Come. We will go to the river and look at the mud. We will find sticky clay. I will put my hands in the clay and I will design a human form who is huge.

MANGOLD: How huge?

RABBI: Nine feet tall.

GOLDMAN: A giant?

RABBI: I will give him a long face, big hands and feet. He will have a large powerful fighter's body.

MANGOLD: I wish I had a fighter's body instead of this miserable little shape. I get beaten up all the time.

RABBI: (*Sings and as he does the GOLEM takes shape.*)
Song:
From the clay
And the earth
From the mud
And the air
I will make this Golem
May he love and protect us
Golem Golem come to me.
(*A shape is seen under a gauze.*)

MANGOLD: Look at that!

RABBI: You will walk seven times around the clay form.

GOLDMAN: The body is red like fire.

MANGOLD: Now I will walk.

GOLDMAN: Seven times.

MANGOLD: The fire is going out in the body.

GOLDMAN: Steam is coming from him.

RABBI: Water and heat that make steam.

GOLDMAN: Oh look the body is growing hair on its head.

MANGOLD: And on the hands there are nails and also on the feet.

GOLDMAN: And he has eyes. Will he open them?

MANGOLD: Will he see us?

GOLDMAN: Will he smell like us?

MANGOLD: And will he sing as sweetly as the man who makes him?

RABBI: And now I walk round seven times...and I will breathe the breath of life into your nostrils and you must take this word into your mouth...E–M–E–T.

MANGOLD: Is that his name?

GOLDMAN: Don't be a schlemiel, schlemiel.

MANGOLD: What's a schlemiel?

GOLDMAN: It's like a nebbish, nebbish.
(*Hits him.*)

RABBI: EMET is the magic word. It means truth... And when I say this magic word EMET then I will put life into your body. EMET. (*Trumpet music.*) Stand on your feet. (*The GOLEM stands. The company are amazed.*)

GOLDMAN: It's incredible!!!

MANGOLD: It is magic!!!

RABBI: Now we will dress you.
(*Everyone dresses the GOLEM in a coat with a yellow patch.*)

GOLDMAN: Do you like that?

MANGOLD: Do you like your coat?

RABBI: The Golem cannot speak.

GOLDMAN: That's a pity.

RABBI: But he understands everything you say.

MANGOLD: What's his name?

RABBI: You are called Joseph. And you have been created to protect us from our enemies, from those who hurt us, Joseph. Stand Joseph. Stand proud.
(*The GOLEM looks at him.*)

RABBI: Walk Golem!

(*Music as GOLEM walks.*)

MANGOLD: You taught him to walk just like that!

RABBI: You are to stay by my side. You are to do all that I
tell you. If I ask you to walk through fire, you will walk
through fire. If I ask you to jump from a tower, you will
jump from a tower. If I ask you to enter deep water, you
will enter deep water. Do you say yes?

(*GOLEM nods.*)

I am calling you Joseph because there once was a Joseph
who had a coat of many colours and he was a good man.
And he helped his people, the people with the yellow
patches too. He helped them when they were far from
home. He helped them when they were in danger.

GOLDMAN: He wasn't a schlemiel like you.

(*He smacks MANGOLD who smacks him back.*)

RABBI: I want you to be a good man and help all of us in
our coats of yellow patches.

GOLDMAN: But how will we explain who the Golem is to
the rest of the people?

RABBI: We will say he is a poor man who cannot talk that
we have found in the forest. We will say that we felt
sorry for him and have taken him into our house. It is
good to take in a stranger, a foreigner.

GOLDMAN: Can you remember that schlemiel?

MANGOLD: Don't call me a schlemiel.

RABBI: Now Golem, chop the wood, carry our water from
the well, clean our houses. Go shlep.

MANGOLD: What is shlep?

RABBI: Shlep means drag. For example I have to shlep
over to the well to get the water. But now the Golem will
shlep to the well for all of us.

(*Everyone applauds the RABBI as the GOLEM carries out
the work. Pogrom music suggesting the danger is about to
arrive.*)

RABBI: Now Golem, defend us with your strength.

MANGOLD: Oh no. Look the people without the yellow
patches, they are coming. I am scared. They will tear up
the rabbi's magic books. They will hurt us.

(*Music. The GOLEM beats the rabble.*)

GOLDMAN: Look! Look at the Golem. He is angry with the men who come to hurt us. He is our hero. Our superman. Now we have our Golem nobody will harm us. Now we have our Golem we are strong. Now we have our Golem nobody can ever beat us up.

MANGOLD: Now we are all somebody because of the magic performed by the Rabbi.

GOLDMAN: Rabbi you are a magician.

MANGOLD: A magician of magicians. Now our enemies will see that yes we we love learning but we also we know how to fight.

(*The GOLEM playfully lifts up GOLDMAN. Knockabout music.*)

GOLDMAN: Hey, hey. Stop that. Put me down.

(*The GOLEM drops him. He does a prat fall.*)

MANGOLD: Now we have a hero. We can have peace!

RABBI: And if we have peace I hope one day to dance at your wedding.

GOLDMAN: My wedding? First our grandmother must get married.

RABBI: Yes.

MANGOLD: And our parents.

RABBI: Yes.

GOLDMAN: And then we can be born.

(*The GOLEM watches the puppet BRIDE, intently. He grabs her and does a long crazed dance to wild music.*)

RABBI: Golem. Stop now!

(*He takes the doll from the GOLEM who yells in agony.*)

MANGOLD: Poor Golem. Poor nebbish.

GOLDMAN: He doesn't feel anything. He's not human.

MANGOLD: Then why is he crying?

GOLDMAN: Yes Rabbi. Why is he crying?

RABBI: Maybe I made him too human. I tell him off and he cries.

(*The GOLEM tries to take grab the BRIDE.*)

No. Golem, I told you no.

(*The GOLEM whimpers like a puppy.*)

GOLDMAN: He has a voice.

RABBI: But he cannot talk.

MANGOLD: Why can't he talk?

RABBI: Because he has no soul.

GOLDMAN: What is a soul?

RABBI: A soul is something you can't see.

MANGOLD: So what is it?

RABBI: It's something we all have inside. It's what makes you human.

MANGOLD: I have a soul?

RABBI: Yes.

GOLDMAN: Me too?

RABBI: Even you.

GOLDMAN: Only the Golem.

MANGOLD: Has…

RABBI: No soul. Poor Golem.

> (*Music. MANGOLD juggles and throws balls to GOLEM who catches them and finally throws the lot at MANGOLD. This is a tender moment of play between the three.*
> *Music changes. GOLEM sees the RABBI's book and makes a grab for it.*)

No Joseph. You cannot have that book. That is the book that made you.

> (*GOLEM hangs on to the book.*)

Only those who learn can read the book. Only those with wisdom can read the book.

> (*GOLEM refuses to release the book.*)

This is the book of magic. That is the book that has all the knowledge in the world.

> (*RABBI seizes the book. Attack from outside.*
> *Drumming noise. It is a pogrom. All cast hold hands and are downstage. They walk slowly upstage without turning their backs.*)

GOLDMAN: What is happening?

MANGOLD: The people, the people with the plain coats, they are coming back to hurt us.

GOLDMAN: Grandmother, Golem, Rabbi what can we do?

RABBI: Golem, I order you to protect us and fight our enemies. But nobody must die.

> (*The GOLEM defends his people. The attackers disappear.*)

Good Golem. You are a good Golem. I am glad you hurt nobody.

(*The GOLEM smiles, and takes a swipe at the RABBI.*)

No. Not me. You don't fight me. I can see I shall have to watch you.

(*The GOLEM turns away in shame.*)

GOLDMAN: Rabbi. The sun has vanished.

RABBI: It has been a long day. Let's sleep.

(*RABBI, GOLDMAN and MANGOLD sleep. The GOLEM watches them.*)

I am dreaming. I see pictures. I see stars. I see heavens. I see angels.

GOLDMAN: I am dreaming too! I am in the room without windows. The room without doors.

MANGOLD: Me too. I am dreaming. Dreaming of Queen Esther protecting her people from danger.

GOLDMAN: I am dreaming of Solomon. Of Sheba. In Africa. A–F–R–I–C–A. Ethiopia.

MANGOLD: Ethiopia. People with long locks.

RABBI: I see a tree. No it's a bush. Ah there's a fire. A burning bush. I see a Golden Calf. I see people dancing all round it. I am in a lion's den. I can see the writing on the wall.

MANGOLD: And Solomon was a wise king.

RABBI: The question is, when I dream, is that real or when I am awake is that real?

(*The GOLEM has come towards the sleeping RABBI and tries to attack him. He runs in a panic. He tries to pick up the BRIDE.*)

Stop it now.

GOLDMAN: You put my grandmother down!

MANGOLD: Don't you touch my our grandmother or I'll do something!

GOLDMAN: Oh so she's your grandmother too is she?

MANGOLD: You promised I could share her.

GOLDMAN: Oh alright.

RABBI: Put her down Golem. (*The GOLEM holds on.*) I order you Golem. (*Slowly the GOLEM puts her down.*) You are to obey me, do you hear? (*The GOLEM paws the*

ground in resistance.) Only me. (*The GOLEM makes one
more try to grab the BRIDE.*)

(*RABBI is outraged.*) Genug iz genug!

GOLDMAN: Enough is enough.

RABBI: He has turned against me. I made him from
nothing and now he tries to destroy me.

MANGOLD: Why does he do that?

RABBI: (*To GOLEM.*) Go to your room (*GOLEM stares back
defiantly.*) Geh. Shluf.

GOLDMAN: Go. Sleep. He doesn't want to go to bed. He
thinks it is too early. He wants to stay up and have fun.

RABBI: Go to your room. I order you! Now! (*GOLEM
won't move.*) Go to your room! Go to your room! Go to
your room! Go to your room!

MANGOLD: Read him a story, rabbi, that'll make him sleep.

RABBI: Sleep!

MANGOLD: Oh I am so tired. (*Yawns and pretends to sleep
snoring to encourage the GOLEM. The problem is he really
does fall asleep while the GOLEM remains awake.
GOLDMAN kicks MANGOLD awake.*)

GOLDMAN: Not you silly!

MANGOLD: Oh did I fall asleep?

RABBI: Golem. Sleep!

(*He sings these lyrics to Brahms lullaby.*)

Shluf mein kind

Shluf mein kind

sleep is on the wind

stars will glimmer

eyes get dimmer

and your fears are all long gone

don't be scared of the dark

close to you we will mark

all is calm

still and calm

and there won't be more harm.

(*The GOLEM is asleep.*)

GOLDMAN: You've got me sleepy too. I am dreaming of
grandma. Isn't it time she got married?

RABBI: Married?

GOLDMAN: Now we have peace again. Now we can have weddings again. Now our grandmother can marry our grandfather. They can have our parents. And we can be born.

MANGOLD: But we are born silly! We are here. (*Hits him.*) Did you feel that?

GOLDMAN: But even that could be in a dream. Maybe not my dream. Maybe grandma is dreaming us? Maybe we only exist in her dreams. And when you hit me it is in grandma's dream. Maybe we are in her room without windows, without doors?

RABBI: Never mind who's dreaming we still have work to do.

MANGOLD: What work?

GOLDMAN: But it's bedtime.

(*RABBI clicks his fingers. GOLDMAN and MANGOLD become alert.*)

RABBI: I made this Golem to save us but he turns against me. I made him to fight and now he fights me. I made a mistake in thinking I could control him. (*Beat.*) To make the Golem I walked from right to left and to unmake the Golem I will walk from left to right. Again I say the magic word. E–M–E–T.

(*Music. Slowly the GOLEM disappears under the gauze... Only his coat remains.*)

GOLDMAN: Where is he?

MANGOLD: Where did he go?

RABBI: He went back into earth and water and fire. He went back into the air.

GOLDMAN: Why did you make him vanish rabbi?

MANGOLD: We loved him.

GOLDMAN: That's right. He protected us. Now we have nobody at all to fight our battles for us. When the people without the yellow patches come to kill us what shall we do?

MANGOLD: He is right. You gave us a hero and then you took him away. Why did you make him vanish?
(*Stamping foot like a child.*) Golem now! Golem now! Golem now!

GOLDMAN: I thought you didn't want a Golem.

MANGOLD: That was then. This is now. It's not fair.

RABBI: Nothing in life is fair.

GOLDMAN: Why did you destroy the Golem?

RABBI: I made a mistake.

MANGOLD: A mistake?

RABBI: I made him to protect us from our enemies.

MANGOLD: Yes!

RABBI: But Joseph Golem went out of control.

GOLDMAN: He didn't mean to.

RABBI: I couldn't take the risk. I made him from the earth
and the fire and the water. And what I made was
dangerous.

GOLDMAN: It was magic, it was wonderful and now it's all
gone.

RABBI: When I decided to make him, I was wrong.

GOLDMAN: Not wrong.

RABBI: A mistake.

MANGOLD: No.

RABBI: A man can learn from his mistake.

GOLDMAN: What did you learn?

RABBI: I learned that we all have the Golem inside us.

MANGOLD: Inside us?

RABBI: In our own room without windows our own room
without doors.

MANGOLD: I want to go to that room.

GOLDMAN: Where do I find it?

MANGOLD: Where has he gone? Where has Joseph Golem
gone?

RABBI: Into you. Into me. (*Beat.*) You have to stand up for
yourself now.

GOLDMAN: But how? I am weak.

MANGOLD: And so am I. And you are hardly made of
muscles.

RABBI: You see that coat?

MANGOLD: The Golem's coat? He left it behind.

GOLDMAN: (*To himself and to the audience.*) Which is worse
a man without a coat or a coat without a man?

RABBI: A man without a coat? He is so cold. A coat
without a man, it is so empty.

RABBI: When the next attack comes, I want you to take a piece of the cloth and put it next to your heart.

MANGOLD: Why?

GOLDMAN: Are you meschuggah? Have you gone mad?

RABBI: Try.

(*GOLDMAN and MANGOLD take a piece of cloth from the GOLEM's coat and put it in their breast pockets.*)

GOLDMAN: I feel... (*He starts to grow.*)

MANGOLD: I feel rather strange. (*He too grows.*)

RABBI: What do you feel?

GOLDMAN: (*Laughs and begins to roar.*) I feel strong. I feel strong for the first time in my life.

MANGOLD: So do I. I feel tall, tall like the Golem. (*He laughs.*) Nobody can hurt me now.

GOLDMAN: I can feel my muscles. I can feel the blood flowing through my arms and my legs. I can feel my brain working. I can go anywhere and do anything.

MANGOLD: Rabbi what have you done?

RABBI: It is not I but you. You have let the strength of the Golem enter into you and you will use this power wisely and with intelligence.

GOLDMAN: (*To the BRIDE.*) Shall we bring grandmother with us?

MANGOLD: Yes because now we are now all safe and the Golem is inside us.

RABBI: So let the bride be married!

(*He circles her seven times while GOLDMAN and MANGOLD pretend to be strong men. Music. Outside there is a rumbling as the people try and attack the group. GOLDMAN and MANGOLD show their muscles and fearlessly prime themselves for a fight. The danger passes.*)

(*RABBI gives parts of the coat to the audience.*)

Take a little of the Golem's strength inside each one of you and that way you will be able to fight when you need to. (*Beat.*) Look night is falling, the sky is red. Tomorrow will be a fine day.

(*In longing.*) G–o–l–e–m!

(*Blackout.*)

The End.

YEAR ZERO

to Ian Watts

Why I wrote Year Zero and St Joan

I was living in Maubeuge and the north of France over the 1990s. My husband was the Socialist Mayor of Maubeuge and I went with him to several memorial meetings held by former soldiers. Gradually, I became aware of the weight of experience of those who had been part of twentieth century French history. The occupation of France was still fresh in the memory of many. I interviewed those who had been collaborators, black marketeers, Communists, Gaullists and French women who had been children witnessing prostitutes and mothers getting their heads shaved for 'horizontal collaboration'. Poignantly, the daughter of a collaborating policeman, murdered by the Resistance in 1944, begged me to remove from my play the incident which revealed her father's treachery. The past pushed into the present and the production provoked feelings of unease in Maubeuge which preferred to forget its past.

St Joan was also inspired by the life I led in Maubeuge. I was frequently taken for an Algerian Arab and, when I said I was a Jew, direct antisemitism was expressed. At this time I learnt that Joan of Arc was the icon of the extreme Right in France and I felt moved to write an alternative modern Joan to give voice to those 'outsiders' in French society. My Joan is a modern Jewish Black woman who satirises notions of national purity. The play provoked fury from neo-Nazis in London and Paris and I received death threats on the web and by telephone. In Paris the theatre filled with the very people who rarely go to the theatre. The Blacks, the Arabs, the youth who find theatre has nothing to say to them. I was told 'no French person would dare write this'.

Characters

The Clowns:

MARIANNE DE PARIS

MARIANNE DE VICHY

PUNCH

JUDY

GENDARME

MASTER OF CEREMONIES

The Soldiers:

TOMMY
a British soldier

JULES
a French soldier

The Resistance:

JACQUES
a French volunteer for work in Germany

PIERRE
a Communist

RENARD
a Communist

GUILLAUME
a Communist

SONIA
a ballet dancer working for the resistance

The Collaborators:

YVONNE

HENRI

THE WOMAN WITH THE SHAVED HEAD

COMMISSAIRE OF THE POLICE

MARIE
a double agent

Workers:

THE TOWN HALL DOCTOR

MICHEL
a man who does not want to go to Germany

NEWSBOY

FRANÇOIS

Extras:

JOSEPHINE
a prostitute

CHANTAL
a prostitute

PROSTITUTE'S LITTLE GIRL

A MADAME

MILITARY PROSECUTOR

DEFENCE LAWYER

A MOTHER

YOUNG MARIANNE
her daughter

With doubling, the play can be performed
with a minimum of eight actors.
Year Zero is set in a small northern
French town between 1940 and 1945.

Original ensemble:

JULES / HEAD OF THE RESISTANCE /
GENDARME / DOCTOR / LAWYER, Jerôme Bigo

JACQUES ROUSSEAU / ALBERT RENARD /
HENRI DUCLOS / POLICEMAN, Thomas Desfosses

PUNCH / PRIEST ONE / FRANÇOIS THE
FOREMAN / NEWSAPER BOY, Stéphane Titelein

MASTER OF CEREMONIES / DOCTOR / TOMMY/
CHIEF OF POLICE, Bruno Tuchzer

MARIANNE DE PARIS / A PROSTITUTE /
WOMAN WITH THE SHAVED HEAD,
Véronique Arbez

THE ACCORDIANIST / YVONNE CLEMENT /
A PROSTITUTE, Mathilde Braure

THE DANCER ACROBAT / JUDY / SONIA / THE
LITTLE GIRL IN THE BROTHER / YOUNG
MARIANNE, Laure Smadja

MARIANNE DE VICHY / A PROSTITUTE,
Marie-Odile Sahajdak

Décor and Choreography, Thomas Kampe

Lighting Designer, Ian Watts

At the Cambridge performances Philippe Smolikowski and
Juliet Dante took over the roles of Henri and Yvonne.

Thomas Kampe's design used screens on wheels which were
pushed by the company giving a merry go round set of moving
tableaux setting up the style of the play. This should be a
mixture of circus, knockabout, cabaret and naturalism. The
popular songs chosen are from the period and illustrate or
counterpoint the politics.

Scene 1
The Funfair

Drum roll. Spotlight.

MASTER OF CEREMONIES: Roll up, roll up. Come and
see all the fun of the war. See heroes and villains, girls
who give pleasure and virtuous wives, honest men and
black marketeers. See a small town, somewhere on the
border, somewhere near England, somewhere near
Belgium, somewhere near Germany – let's call it
Maubeuge. See a small one-time garrison town where
Louis XIV's ramparts tried to keep the foreigners out
and failed miserably.
See the pure French who have Dutch, Spanish, English
and German blood in their veins.
Roll up, roll up. We have important men. Over here in
Munich we have Adolph shaking hands with Neville.
And here is Joe shaking hands – again with Adolph.
Doesn't he get around dear Adolph! It's so nice to see
statesmen getting on.
Roll up. Roll up. Come and see the shooting range.
Have a shot at Alsasce Lorraine. Now it's French. And
now – bull's eye – it's German!
Wir sprechen französische. Wir sprechen Deutsch.
But ladies and gentlemen – what will we speak
tomorrow?
But then, who cares as long as there's plenty of German
sausage for everyone.
Roll up, roll up, ladies and gentlemen and shake hands
with our great world statesmen.
See how a humble artisan, a man of the people, a
socialist; that is a national socialist; becomes
Reichschancellor.
What an artist is our Adolph. He's an immigrant from
Austria but don't tell anyone. He likes to travel. To see
the world. He likes building roads so that others can
travel. Oh yes indeed, he's a very friendly chappie.
Watch him shake hands with dear old Neville over here

in Munich. Watch him shake hands with that Georgian
bear Uncle Joe.

Oh dear, poor Germany! She's been forced to invade
Czechoslovakia.

Did I say invade? I mean she's been forced to defend
herself against all those churlish Czechs.

You know how troublesome East Europeans are. And
look over here in Poland. Again plucky little Prussians
forced to defend themselves against those provocative
Poles.

Slavs...never trust them.

And now Denmark. Poor Adolf, forced once again to
enter foreign territory, well he needs the space – all that
empty space in Scandinavia – and now moving towards
home, la belle France.

What have we here, ladies and gentlemen? Take your
rifles, load the barrel and get ready to aim because it's
war!

No it's not, it's the phoney war, quelle drole de guerre,
watch French men wait patiently on the Maginot Line
while Jerry enters by the back door.

And here in the sleepy little town of Maubeuge see a
whole city razed to the ground.

Roll up, roll up, ladies and gentlemen and see the naked
lady (*Beat.*) completely dressed.

(*MARIANNE DE VICHY comes on stage.*)

Watch Miss France try to hold on to her title.

(*MARIANNE DE PARIS comes on stage. The MASTER OF
CEREMONIES gives them boxing gloves. The bell rings.
MARIANNE DE PARIS and MARIANNE DE VICHY box.*)

Since 1789, Marianne de Paris has held on to her title as
Miss France almost uninterruptedly. Now a new
contender comes in for the kill and it's Marianne de
Vichy.

(*MARIANNE DE VICHY knocks out MARIANNE DE
PARIS. The MASTER OF CEREMONIES counts out
MARIANNE DE PARIS who tries valiantly to stand.
MARIANNE DE VICHY raises up her arms in victory.*)

And it's Marianne de Vichy who is the out and out winner in the first round.

And her coach is:

MARIANNE DE VICHY: (*Kisses photos of Papa Pétain and Hitler. These are hung by the MASTER OF CEREMONIES.*) Papa Pétain and Uncle Addie!

MASTER OF CEREMONIES: And poor Marianne de Paris will have to go back to her training.

(*He takes a pigeon out of a top hat. MARIANNE DE VICHY takes out a gun and shoots. A man in a top hat enters smoking a cigar. A second man enters wearing a De Gaulle Képi.*)

MARIANNE DE PARIS: Help Papa Winnie and Charlie.

(*Each kisses her hand. They give her a phrygian bonnet.*)

MASTER OF CEREMONIES: Oh it's sad, ladies and gentlemen, sad to lose the crown but it's a pleasure to announce a new winner!

Marianne de Vichy, what have you got to say about your fight?

MARIANNE DE VICHY: I had very good training from old Papa Pétain and Uncle Addie. Without them I'd still be back in the gym hitting a punchball.

(*Two men raise her arms in a fascist salute.*)

MASTER OF CEREMONIES: And Marianne de Paris, what have you got to say about finally losing the title?

MARIANNE DE PARIS: (*Snarling.*) I'm going back to the gym and when I'm good and ready I'll knock her teeth in.

MASTER OF CEREMONIES: As the English say, ladies and gentlemen, you should always be a good loser. And they should know, ha ha!

So there you have it, ladies and gentlemen. Roll up and see the show because, like the Windmill Girls, our show never stops!

Scene 2
Dance Interlude

Offenbach's can-can music played at correct tempo and then slowly distorted. Both MARIANNES dance.

Scene 3
Song Interlude

MARIANNE DE VICHY sings 'Tout va très bien Madame la Marquise'. MARIANNE DE PARIS sings 'Oh Tommy'. Gunfire, bombing, marching feet, German voices, Hitler, sirens, Charles de Gaulle's broadcast from the BBC 18 June 1940 'Ici Londres'.

Bring back the Offenbach very slowly; as the women are dancing in half-light the following scene is played out.

Scene 4
Dunkirk

Water splashing half-light: men in a boat.

ENGLISH VOICE: Get out, we're full, we can't take any more.

FRENCH VOICE: For God's sake, let me stay, they'll kill me.

ENGLISH VOICE: I told you get out we're full. Hide and you'll be alright.

FRENCH VOICE: I told you they'll kill me. One more won't make a difference.

ENGLISH VOICE: Sorry mate, we're already overloaded. We got orders. English army first and then French. Sorry mate.

(Splash.)

FRENCH VOICE ONE: Oh shit, oh shit.

FRENCH VOICE TWO: Comrade? Can you row?

FRENCH VOICE ONE: Try me.

FRENCH VOICE TWO: Comrade, can you row without oars?

FRENCH VOICE ONE: Try me.

FRENCH VOICE TWO: If you don't want your holidays in Dunkirk we'll row to England with our hands.

FRENCH VOICE ONE: Put our hands in La Manche, why not?

(*Sounds of water splashing. Schubert's 'The Trout' is sung in German and then in French.*)

Scene 5
Call Up

MARIANNE DE VICHY: Get to know Germany better. Today Germany is at the centre of world events. Lots of foreigners would like to get to know this new Germany: Adolf Hitler's Germany. It's very easy. Join the French Voluntary Unit in the fight against Bolshevism. Join the Artillery and the Infantry.

Conditions of employment are open to former soldiers and young men of nineteen and older. Earn three hundred and sixty francs a month with free lodging, plenty of good nourishing food and a daily tobacco allocation – all free.

All you need is permission from your father and your doctor.

Scene 6
The Town Hall
Voluntary Labour – The Medical

The Town Hall. DOCTOR is examining men who are to be sent to Germany to work.

DOCTOR: Next.

JACQUES: Good morning doctor.

DOCTOR: Name?

JACQUES: Rousseau. Jacques.

DOCTOR: No relation?

JACQUES: To who?

DOCTOR: Jean-Jacques.

JACQUES: Who?

DOCTOR: Oh never mind. (*Beat.*) Profession?

JACQUES: Railway worker.

DOCTOR: Age?

JACQUES: Twenty-four.

DOCTOR: You don't look a day over forty.

JACQUES: What?

DOCTOR: Health?

JACQUES: (*Proudly.*) Never had a day's sick in my life. Even in school never missed a day. Not even flu during the epidemic. (*DOCTOR thumps him in the back.*) Jesus Christ. What you do that for? (*Coughs.*)

DOCTOR: Lungs playing up.

JACQUES: You winded me.

DOCTOR: (*With ear to chest.*) Let's have a listen.

JACQUES: Never even had a cold.

DOCTOR: Pneumonia.

JACQUES: (*Aghast.*) What?

DOCTOR: Double bronchial pneumonia.

JACQUES: You're having me on.

DOCTOR: Three months bed-rest.

JACQUES: What?

DOCTOR: Smoke do you?

JACQUES: (*Takes out a packet.*) Want one?

DOCTOR: Filthy habit. (*Knocks them out of JACQUES' hand.*) Stains the teeth. Yellows the fingers. Makes the breath stink.

JACQUES: My lungs doctor, bronchial pneumonia, you're not serious?

DOCTOR: Rotten.

JACQUES: (*Horrified.*) Rotten? (*Beat.*) And Germany. I need the money, there's no work here.

DOCTOR: Permission to go to Germany denied.

JACQUES: Shit. Oh doctor. I was looking forward to it. Make new friends. Make some money...know what I mean.

(*DOCTOR hits him on the back and sends him flying.*)

DOCTOR: Next.

MICHEL: Good morning doctor. My liver's in a terrible state.

DOCTOR: Permission to go to Germany denied. Next.

(*The MASTER OF CEREMONIES and MARIANNE DE VICHY sing 'Amusez Vous'.*)

Scene 7
Prison Cell (1)

TOMMY and JULES in a cell in Germany. TOMMY, the British soldier, is singing 'It's a Long Way To Tipperary'. It's dawn. The two men have been sleeping badly.

JULES: Tommy? Bonjour Tommy.

TOMMY: Bonjour comrade. What's it for you then. Bacon, egg, toast, cup of tea?

JULES: Tu as dormi?

TOMMY: Impossible to dormi with a git that's moaning all night.

JULES: Comment?

TOMMY: Impossible to get shut-eye when French's moaning all night.

JULES: Excuse-moi, Tommy. A nighthorse. Bad dreams. Avez vous une cigarette?

TOMMY: No thanks. I've given up. (*Sings.*) Pack up your troubles in your old kit bag and smile smile smile.

JULES: Tomorrow I am finished.

TOMMY: No.

JULES: Vous êtes croyant?

TOMMY: What's that when it's at home? Quoi?

JULES: Dieu. (*Mimes praying.*) You?

TOMMY: Am I a Christian?

JULES: Oui.

TOMMY: No, I'm a bleedin' Red.

JULES: Quoi? Red? Rouge? Communist?

TOMMY: Yeh, commie bastard. That's me.

JULES: Me non.

TOMMY: You believe in God?

JULES: God. No. De Gaulle maybe.

TOMMY: Charles de Gaulle. Winston Churchill. Uncle Joe
Stalin. Uncle bleedin' Adolph. All the same mate. All
have your balls for breakfast.

JULES: Breakfast? Bacon and eggs.

TOMMY: Listen. Écoute. De Gaulle. Old Charlie.
Churchill. Stalin. Hitler. All the same. Pareil mate.

JULES: You a Communist and you say that?

TOMMY: What do they all want? Qu'est-ce qu'ils veulent?
Tous?

JULES: Breakfast?

TOMMY: Power mate. Le pouvoir.

JULES: Oui, mais avec de Gaulle en pouvoir, moi, je ne
suis pas mort.

TOMMY: You got a point. Vous avez raison camarade. Vous
avez raison. The problem is they send us out to do their
dirty work for them. Ils nous envoyent faire leur
saloperie pour eux pendant qu'ils dorment bien dans un
lit avec une petite chérie à leur côté. And we ain't got a
little darling next to us. All we got is frozen balls.

JULES: 'Frozen ball'?

TOMMY: That's right mate. Nous avons des couilles gelées.

JULES: Ou êtes-vous né?

TOMMY: Where was I born? London town. You know
where London is comrade?

JULES: 'Ici Londres. Ici Londres.' Aujourd'hui c'est mon
anniversaire.

TOMMY: Happy birthday to you, you were born in a zoo.
With the monkeys and the donkeys, happy birthday to
you. (*Scratching.*) How can fleas survive this cold? (*Beat.*)
Twenty-one and still a virgin. Vingt-et-une et encore une
vierge.

JACQUES: Is that what they say in England?

TOMMY: You remember your first time?

JULES: The first time with a girl?

TOMMY: I hope you don't prefer boys?

JULES: I'll never see my wife Yvonne again. The bosch will kill me today.

TOMMY: You said that yesterday and you're still here.

Scene 8
A Clean Sweep

MARIANNE DE VICHY: (*Sweeping the stage.*) Tuberculosis, cancer, syphilis – these are all curable today. But we've got to get rid of the biggest plague of all – the Jew.

MASTER OF CEREMONIES: It's good to see a woman cleaning her house don't you think ladies and gentlemen. (*Uses the brush as a rifle.*)

Now we're at peace with our friendly soldaten, it's time to tidy up, don't you think. Paris. Paris. Paris. That golden city of joy. Aren't we going to make our German guests welcome in Paris? Show a bit of leg Marianne de Vichy. They've not just come here to take the waters. (*MARIANNE DE VICHY dances with a German soldier singing 'Sympathie'.*)

Roll up, ladies and gentlemen, roll up, all the fun of the fair...

Scene 9
Punch and Judy (1)

Two actors in conventional costume. PUNCH has a sword and a baton.

PUNCH: Judy, Judy, Judy. How can a Frenchman be a Frenchman and a Jew at the same time?

JUDY: I don't know, Punch, how can a Frenchman be a Frenchman and a Jew at the same time?

PUNCH: (*To audience.*) She doesn't know. Aren't women stupid. I mean she doesn't know. He can't. (*Hits her.*) Especially if his name is Dreyfus. (*Breaks sword in two.*)

JUDY: Now why have you done that Punch? It was a
   perfectly good sword.

PUNCH: So I can hit you harder like every wife deserves.
   (*Beat.*) Judy, Judy, Judy. Let's see how clever you are.
   Even a woman has some brain if she only keeps it in her
   knickers.

   Judy, Judy, Judy – how many Jewish judges have we got
   today in our beautiful country on this sunny July day in
   the Year of Our Lord nineteen-hundred and forty-one?

JUDY: I don't know Punch.

PUNCH: Ladies and gentleman. She doesn't know. (*Smack.*)
   Guess Judy. Guess. Try and use that little brain of yours.
   Guess.

JUDY: I don't know. Two hundred.

PUNCH: No. (*Smack.*) Try again.

JUDY: Fifty. (*He hits her until she's almost dead.*)

PUNCH: No ladies and gentlemen. Isn't that just like a
   woman. Ignorant. Pig ignorant.
   How many Jewish judges? How many Jewish
   magistrates? How many Jewish teachers? How many
   Jewish actors? How many Jewish editors?
   Guess Judy. Guess.

JUDY: I don't know. Tell me Punch.

PUNCH: The answer ladies and gentleman is (*Laughs.*) –
   NONE!

JUDY: And how many people protested at this ban?

PUNCH: How many people protested? What are we,
   protestants?
   Ladies and gentlemen, she thinks she's an intellectual.
   She can't even vote and she thinks she's an intellectual!
   Well, Judy, since you ask how many people protested
   against this ban the answer is – I have to tell you –
   NONE!!
   (*He smacks her for no reason at all.*)
   Judy, have you heard of our saviour, Maréchal Pétain?
   (*He gives the fascist salute.*)

JUDY: He's a friend of Monsieur Adolf.

PUNCH: Good girl Judy. Well since you're my one and
   only wife I have to tell you also that you've won the new

slogan. Travail. Famille. Patrie. Repeat after me. Travail. Famille. Patrie.

(*JUDY is silent.*)

What! You dare to disobey me? (*Smack.*)

I'll have to look in to this. I'll have to look in to your background. (*Beat.*)

You've got a big nose!

Ladies and gentlemen, hasn't she got a big nose?

JUDY: Like General de Gaulle?

PUNCH: (*Smack.*) Don't you mention that name here.

No we'll have to look into your background. What's your name? Jew-dy? Isn't that short for Judith? Isn't that a Jewish name?

Scene 10
Prison Cell (2)

Dogs bark in the near distance.

JULES: Work? London? You?

TOMMY: My job? I was a tailor. Schneider. Tailleur.

JULES: My tailor is rich.

TOMMY: Not me mate. Pas riche.

JULES: (*Practising his English.*) My tailor is rich. Once I met a Jew. In Cambrai. He made me a suit. Tu es juif? You Jew?

TOMMY: My family escaped the pogroms. They bought a boat ticket for America. When they arrived they heard English. When they discovered where they were it was too late. Pity. I should've been an American.

JULES: My papa. He died at Ypres.

TOMMY: Where?

JULES: Ypres.

TOMMY: My father was in the trenches. Only he was at Wipers. Gassed. (*Beat.*) What you here for?

JULES: Sabotage.

TOMMY: That's English. Sabotage.

JULES: Sabotage de pylon.

TOMMY: Good work comrade.

JULES: Et tu?

TOMMY: Dodgy landing.

JULES: Quoi?

TOMMY: Parachute.

JULES: Airman.

TOMMY: Airman. Luftmann.

JULES: Tu parles allemand?

TOMMY: (*Yiddish.*) Ein bissel. Comme ci, comme ça.

JULES: Et alors?

TOMMY: A mademoiselle found me. On a farm. Normandy somewhere. Good food. Good plonk.

JULES: Plonk?

TOMMY: Vin blanc. Plonk.

JULES: Chablis.

TOMMY: No Normandy. She was a real smasher. A real dish.

JULES: You like French girls?

TOMMY: (*Salutes.*) Oui mon colonel.

JULES: And how were you captured?

TOMMY: Someone blew the whistle on me. They took us both. I haven't seen her since.

JULES: Un oiseau a chanté.

TOMMY: Too right. A little bird sang alright.

JULES: You have a cigarette?

TOMMY: No thanks. I've given up.

(*Dogs bark in the near distance but louder than before.*)

Scene 11
A Naval Interlude

MARIANNE DE VICHY is still sweeping while MARIANNE DE PARIS is training in the corner.

The company sings 'Les Gars de la Marine'.

The jolliness is smashed midflow as a newsboy shouts from the street corner while the company leave.

NEWSBOY: Paris Soir! Paris Soir! Mers El Klebir. Churchill bombs French fleet. One thousands nine

hundred and twenty-three French sailors killed.
(*Cross fade in to next scene.*)

Scene 12

SONIA, a ballet dancer, is on tour in Lyons. Her job makes her an ideal person to pass messages and packets to the resistance. She has been arrested and is being tortured by Klaus Barbie. To stop the pain she talks to herself to stop herself from naming names. This scene can be done as part dance.

SONIA: Guten Tag Herr Barbie. Yes you are a real bastard. Go on. Hit me as much as you like. Harder. Oh God, how will I stop myself talking. If only there wasn't such pain. Maybe I will pass out and if I talk they won't hear me. Die Namen. Die Anderen. No I won't say who they are. I won't speak their names. How am I going to stop myself? Think of something else. The routine. After the show when I have finished my act. Someone will come to my dressing room. He'll ask for my autograph. And he will give me a packet. No think of something else. The routine. My first ballet classes. Au dessous. Over. En dessous. Under. Put the stuff under the bridge. Sauter. To jump. Make the train jump off the rails. Make the pylon jump high in the sky. Yes!!! Plier. To bend. Plier plus bas. Bend lower. When you bend your knees make sure the top of your head doesn't move. Top. Top dog. Top him. Top the collaborator. Un battement. Beat the leg. Beating me. Un grand battement. A massive beating. Chassé. Pourchassé. They chased me all over the city. I don't know any name. I don't know anyone in Lyons. I am from the north. I came here to dance. That's all. Think of something else. Now a foutté. And the leg whips round. My God is that really a whip? He's going to whip me 'til I talk. I'll die with the pain. Mother, where are you? One day you taught me a Russian song. What was it?
(*She sings a Russian folk song. As this scene ends and the three men enter for the next scene, a woman takes a postcard and cuts it in two. She gives the two halves to a woman and a man at different moments. Each one takes a packet from her and then leaves the area. A woman sews a priest's soutane.*)

Scene 13
Sabotage

Sound of a steam train passing.

PIERRE, the Chief, and two other men in a room.

PIERRE: Go to the track. Look carefully at how the rail
ends meet. They are fixed with bolts which are secured
into the wood. Look at how they are bolted down. Our
railwaymen will give you the keys to unbolt the
connections. This is your focus. This is where you work.
You'll unbolt with the keys and then lift the portion of
rail shifting it to the side. One portion goes to the right,
the other to the left. Understand?
It's tough. Very tough. At least an hour's work for the
four of you. Never be more than four. Above all work in
complete silence.
The Germans survey night and day.
Occasionally they use kids from the local bin. Be
prepared for this. Take a sweet. They are always half
starved so this will work.
The other alternative is dynamite. We get it from friends
who work the mines. You put a charge where the points
meet. Then you need another, at a distance of three and a
half metres. Not less. Never less. Three and a half metres
is the distance between each set of wheels. Obviously
you've got to work at night...the trains are coming from
the Atlantic Wall, jam-packed with Jerry going on his
holidays.
Don't tell the others that the train is full of Jerry. Tell
them it's bomb parts. If they've got their wits about them
they'll know that's impossible. Spare parts arrive from
the east. If they think Jerry's aboard there's more chance
of a foul-up. We know from experience that our boys
instinctively don't like killing Jerry-on-holiday. That's
when they make mistakes. We can't afford this. The
operation must be perfect. One hundred per cent perfect.
If not Jerry has two crackshot machine gunners ready to

blow you to kingdom come. One in the first wagon and one in the last. And when Jerry sees you waiting, the bastard won't give you a chance in hell.

(*Sound of train whistle. Dynamite explosion.*)

Scene 14
The Factory

The company is working in a light industry factory near Aulnoye. Establish mechanical rhythm. YVONNE stops, stretches, yawns. The others continue. HENRI returns and looks at her. He offers her a cigarette. She takes it and he lights it for her. They smile. The others continue working through the scene. He kisses her.

YVONNE: Not now. Not here.

HENRI: I couldn't help it. You're delicious. The smell of your skin drives me mad.

YVONNE: Later.

HENRI: When?

YVONNE: When it's dark.

HENRI: That late. I may die of longing.

YVONNE: Others die. You never.

HENRI: You don't take me seriously.

YVONNE: Let's get back to work.

HENRI: I'm tired of work.

YVONNE: You should be glad to have it. You should be glad you're not over there shovelling earth for thirteen hours a day.

HENRI: I know.

YVONNE: (*She blows smoke out and sighs.*) No trouble for ten days here. Must be a record.

HENRI: That's how I like it best. No trouble.

(*They go back to work.*)

YVONNE: How did you?

HENRI: How did I what?

YVONNE: You know. Manage to stay here when so many went on forced labour.

HENRI: Travelling never appealed much to me. When you've got the best village and the best country, why travel.

YVONNE: I suppose you're right.
HENRI: If I'd gone elsewhere I wouldn't be here with my
     sweetheart. (*Kisses her.*)
YVONNE: The foreman's coming.
HENRI: Then I'll have to wait for tonight.

Scene 15
A Letter to the Commissaire

*MARIANNE DE VICHY writing on the back of MARIANNE DE
PARIS who looks furious.*

MARIANNE DE VICHY: 63 Rue Bourseault XVII, Tel
     Marcadet 5796, Monsieur le Commissaire aux Questions
     Juives à Paris, Monsieur le Commissaire.
     Paris. 20 May 1941.
     Dear Chief of Police for The Jewish Question.
     Thousands of Jews, foreigners and French men have been
     sent to concentration camps. I have nothing to say about
     this as this was an unforeseen effect of the current
     situation. My mother and I needed to have our shoes
     repaired, they are practically new, it's just a question of
     steel tips, so we went to see a cobbler in rue Lemercier. I
     knew nothing about this man except for his reputation as
     a good worker. Last Saturday when I returned to the
     shop what did I find but the shop closed up and the
     cobbler in a concentration camp. What are we supposed
     to do, go out in our slippers!!!!!!!!!!!!!!!!!!!!!!
     Please, accept, dear Sir, our deepest and most
     distinguished greetings.
     Yours faithfully
     Marianne de Vichy also known as Miss France.

Scene 16
The Station

YVONNE: Look in the wagon.
HENRI: I don't believe it.
YVONNE: Well?

HENRI: Tonight it's piano accordions.

YVONNE: You're having me on.

HENRI: A wagon full of piano accordions. Why on earth does Jerry want piano accordions?

YVONNE: Come on let's get out of here. I'm scared.

HENRI: There's nothing to be frightened of.

YVONNE: If they see us.

HENRI: There's nobody here I promise you. You're safe with me. (*Pulls her to him.*) There's only you, me and the accordions.

(*YVONNE laughs. MARIANNE DE VICHY whistles 'Lili Marleen'.*)

Jerry likes music as much as we do.

YVONNE: They're not all bad.

HENRI: They didn't want the war. (*Stroking her.*) It's the Bolsheviks and the Yids who started the war.

YVONNE: (*Responding to his caresses.*) Yes.

HENRI: It's the foreigners who come here who start all the trouble.

YVONNE: (*Getting excited by his caresses.*) Yes.

(*HENRI unbuttons his trousers and pushes her against the wagon. He lifts her dress and the following speeches intercut. Spotlight on YVONNE's face only as he makes thrusting movements in to her. He moves. She doesn't.*)

HENRI: They come here with their smarmy talk and their get rich quick deals because they've all got cousins in America, in the Stock Exchange. They speak several languages because their money controls the world. They pretend to be French men. They speak French like we do. And then you hear them speaking English, German, Russian. Cosmopolitans. They don't know where they belong.

(*Fast lights up on men being machine gunned at the other side of the carriage. They fall. YVONNE lifts her head as if partly conscious of them. HENRI is still pumping in to her. He shudders to a stop and then slumps to the floor exhausted. She looks anxious for a second and then sighs with satisfaction.*)

Scene 17
Punch and Judy (2)

PUNCH: Judy Judy Judy.

JUDY: Yes Punch.

PUNCH: What's the biggest problem of our century?

JUDY: Men?

(*PUNCH whacks JUDY.*)

PUNCH: Women.

JUDY: Women?

PUNCH: That's right, stupid (*Whack.*) women.

JUDY: Why, Punch, why?

PUNCH: Why? Judy. Why? Because you don't have enough children, that's why.

(*JUDY produces children – dolls.*)

Good girl, Judy. Good girl. And you know what you get as a reward?

JUDY: What Punch?

PUNCH: (*Whack.*) A new holiday. Our dear Marshall Pétain has just created a special day for French mothers – Mother's Day. Now isn't that good news? (*Whack.*)

JUDY: Yes, if you say so, Punch.

PUNCH: Judy Judy Judy.

JUDY: Yes Punch.

PUNCH: What's the biggest problem of our century?

JUDY: Men?

PUNCH: Unemployment.

JUDY: That's right. Men. (*Smack.*)

PUNCH: Unemployment leads to violence. (*Smack.*)

JUDY: Yes.

PUNCH: Unemployment leads to crime. (*Smack.*) Do you know how to make thirty million unemployed French men disappear?

JUDY: No Punch.

PUNCH: The answer's easy Judy.

JUDY: How so Punch?

PUNCH: You send them to Germany.

JUDY: To work for Monsieur Adolph?

PUNCH: Or else you send them to Germany and then you
   kill them. (*Smiles.*) That's how you solve the problem of
   all those unemployed Frenchmen.

JUDY: Whose idea is that Punch?

PUNCH: Ladies and gentlemen, we're talking about social
   control and she's asking whose idea is it?

JUDY: Monsieur Adolph's idea?

PUNCH: Well yes, Judy. But he can't do it on his own can
   he. I mean he's busy isn't he. He's got a lot of worries on
   his plate.
   War with England. War with Russia. War in Africa. I
   mean it's not an easy job being Reichschancellor. When
   you advertise for the job, there are very few candidates.

JUDY: I'd take the job.

PUNCH: (*Smack.*) Don't be silly. It's not woman's work. It
   takes a real man to be a Reichschancellor. I mean you've
   got to be prepared to kill millions of people. Poor
   Monsieur Adolph doesn't get much sleep. So he needs
   some help. Now who do you think is going to help him
   here Judy. Try and think.

JUDY: Monsieur Laval? Monsieur Pétain?

PUNCH: Bravo. You're not as thick as you look.

JUDY: But there's something I don't understand Punch.

PUNCH: (*Smack.*) Yes Judy? What don't you understand.

JUDY: If Maréchal Pétain saved the honour of France
   against the Germans in the First World War why is he
   friends with them today?

PUNCH: Haven't you heard about love thy neighbour
   Judy? (*Smack.*)

JUDY: How can the same man be a hero and a traitor at the
   same time?

PUNCH: Look Judy. In the First War he sent 700,000 men
   to their death to defend France and now he's sending
   l00,000 to Germany to reduce the unemployment
   problem here. Seems perfectly logical to me.

JUDY: And that makes him a hero?

PUNCH: The majority of Frenchmen think so and the
   majority is always right – isn't that so Judy. Repeat after
   me. TRAVAILLE, FAMILLE, PATRIE!

(*She is silent. He smacks her.*)

Just like a woman. Never speaks when you want her to and never stops when you want peace.

Listen Judy. Don't you want to be part of the new Europe?

No deviants. (*Smack.*) No criminals. (*Smack.*) No mad people. (*Smack.*) No handicapped. (*Smack.*) No Communists. (*Smack.*) No Socialists. (*Smack.*) No capitalists. No petty bourgeois. No Jews. (*Smack.*) No gypsies. (*Smack.*) No homosexuals. No black marketeers. (*Smack.*) No freemasons. No difficult women (*Smack.*)

JUDY: Who will be left Punch?

PUNCH: Who will be left? Who will be left? The Right. The extreme Right. The extreme Right is always right. (*Enter GENDARME.*)

GENDARME: What have we here?

PUNCH: Bonjour Monsieur Gendarme.

GENDARME: Identity cards.

PUNCH: What?

GENDARME: Identity cards.

PUNCH: (*To JUDY.*) What does he mean?

GENDARME: Marshall Pétain has introduced identity cards for all French men and women.

PUNCH: What for?

GENDARME: What for? Ladies and gentlemen, he asks what for. (*Hits PUNCH with his baton.*) You've got to have identity cards so that we can know who you are. It's the new order. Can't have you wandering around without identity cards can we. Marshall Pétain's orders.

JUDY: I know who I am.

PUNCH: So do I.

GENDARME: But the state needs to know. Don't you like the state?

(*GENDARME raises his baton, smacks PUNCH.*)

PUNCH: Oh don't hit me. Monsieur Gendarme.

GENDARME: Why not? I want to try my new Pétain-baton. (*Smack.*)

PUNCH: Hit her. Hit Judy. Not me. She's used to it.

(*GENDARME pulls down PUNCH's trousers.*)

GENDARME: Are you a Jew?

PUNCH: Not me sir.

(*GENDARME measures PUNCH's skull with a tape measure.*)

GENDARME: One can never be sure these days (*Looks in his mouth.*) Are you a Communist?

PUNCH: No sir.

GENDARME: What are you then?

PUNCH: I'm the same as forty million other Frenchmen.

GENDARME: Oh yes?

PUNCH: I follow our saviour. Maréchal Pétain.

GENDARME: A loyal Frenchman. I'm glad to hear that.

(*PUNCH gives the fascist salute.*)

Get ready then.

PUNCH: (*Offers him a bottle.*) Get ready?

GENDARME: Pack your bag.

PUNCH: I don't understand.

GENDARME: We need loyal men like you for the German war effort.

PUNCH: No, no, no, you don't understand my dear friend. I don't even speak German.

GENDARME: Sprechen Sie Deutsch Herr Punch?

PUNCH: Nein, ich spreche kein Deutsch Herr Polizei.

(*GENDARME produces a suitcase.*)

That's settled then. As long as you don't speak German then we'll send you on an exchange programme. Frenchmen to Germany, Germans to France.

(*PUNCH offers another bottle. The GENDARME takes it and whacks PUNCH. He makes him stand up and forces him to accept his suitcase.*)

JUDY: Bye Punch. Auf wiedersehen. (*She whacks him.*)

Scene 18
Street Scene

NEWSBOY: Extra! Extra! Germans invade Soviet Union. Hitler Stalin Pact kaput.

(*MARIANNE DE VICHY strangles him.*)

RADIO VOICE: (*Off.*) Ici Londres. Ici Londres.

(*MARIANNE DE VICHY makes a sign and the radio waves are blocked out.*)

Scene 19
The Lesson

PIERRE, GUILLAUME, RENARD in a room. They shake hands.

PIERRE: Are you ever afraid? Today I want to talk about fear.

GUILLAUME: Of course.

PIERRE: Good.

RENARD: Why good?

PIERRE: Fear can save your life.

GUILLAUME: How so?

PIERRE: I have a meeting with Monsieur X to establish a liaison in, say, Maubeuge. I get word to make contact with him at la Rotonde opposite La Porte de Mons. Now I don't know anything about Monsieur X except that he will be wearing a check cap and he expects me to be wearing a brown jacket. The rendezvous is on a Wednesday. I receive my orders on a Monday. Monday night I can't sleep. Tuesday night I can't sleep. I'm scared. What do I do when I'm not sleeping? I get up. I drink a coffee. I accept this fear. I let my imagination go for the worst possible scenario. What if he's not reliable? What if he's brought some 'friends' with him? What if he's a double agent. Through my fear I think it through. I make certain decisions.

Instead of arriving for ten I'll get there at eight. And instead of the brown jacket I'll be in my policeman's gabardine and felt hat.

This way I'll be there before him and any 'friends' he might bring with.

This way I'll see them before they see me and I'll be incognito.

And, if for any reason I get the feeling that something's wrong, I'm off and they're still waiting for the guy in the brown jacket.

GUILLAUME: Where can I get a flic's raincoat?

PIERRE: Leave it to me. (*To RENARD.*) You want one too?

RENARD: I'm thinking more about taking holy orders.

Scene 20
For the Love of God

TWO PRIESTS cross one another in the street. They nod. PRIEST TWO is RENARD.

PRIEST ONE: Monsieur.

PRIEST TWO: Monsieur.

PRIEST ONE: Do I know you?

PRIEST TWO: No I'm a stranger in this area.

PRIEST ONE: From which part?

PRIEST TWO: Oh quite a way.

PRIEST ONE: Your accent would make you a man from the northern coast.

PRIEST TWO: Dunkirk.

PRIEST ONE: Oh yes Dunkirk. Ah so you know Abbé Delcroix?

PRIEST TWO: Of course.

PRIEST ONE: How is he?

PRIEST TWO: How is he?

PRIEST ONE: Yes. Improving?

PRIEST TWO: We're praying for his recovery.

PRIEST ONE: A stroke is a terrible thing but the good Lord is with us.

PRIEST TWO: Yes.

PRIEST ONE: And you are Father...?

PRIEST TWO: Benedict.

PRIEST ONE: What's your real name?

PRIEST TWO: I just told you.

PRIEST ONE: (*In Latin.*) *Quisne bellum gallicum vicit?*
[Who won the Gallic Wars?]
Londinium ceu Carthago delendum erit.
[London will fall like Carthage.]
Imposter es.
[And you are an imposter.]

(*Silence.*)

There is no Abbé Delcroix in Dunkirk. The Abbé is called Millet. You're an imposter. Don't you know that it's serious to impersonate a man of God for your own political or criminal ends. As a priest I cannot countenance that.

PRIEST TWO: (*Puts hand in pocket.*) You're right. I'm, not a priest. I don't speak Latin. I speak the language of Karl Marx. Of Vladimir Illich. Joseph Dshugashvili. Lenin. Stalin. Either you're with us and you'll let me go without saying anything to anyone. Or else you're against us and the liberation of France.

I'm armed and I won't hesitate to send a priest to heaven. Or to hell.

So father, you've a decision to make before you see St Peter or the other fella (*Beat.*) I'll count to three. (*Beat.*) One. (*Beat.*) Two. (*Beat.*) Three.

(*Blackout and gunfire.*)

Scene 21
The Factory

The stage is full. Everyone is working.

FRANÇOIS: (*The foreman.*) Stop.

HENRI: What's wrong?

MAN: One of you bastards thinks it's amusing – huh?

HENRI: Ball bearing. Second time this month.

YVONNE: Sabotage.

FRANÇOIS: That's right. It only takes one pure bastard and then we're all at risk.

HENRI: I don't understand. It only makes it rough for all of us.

FRANÇOIS: I want to know who.

HENRI: Why not have a fag and think it over François. I'm sure it'll all become clear with time. (*He motions him to a corner.*) Roger has been acting oddly. I saw him take something out of his pocket about an hour ago.

FRANÇOIS: (*Slaps him on the back.*) Back to work everyone. Let's try and repair the damage. Hey you, yes you. I want a word with you.

(*ROGER walks over to FRANÇOIS and looks at HENRI accusingly.*

The company go back to work.)

YVONNE: I had a message this morning.

HENRI: What?

YVONNE: From Jules.

HENRI: That's impossible.

YVONNE: I thought so too. I just couldn't believe it. A message from a dead man.

HENRI: He's not dead then.

YVONNE: Only if dead men still write.

HENRI: Where is he?

YVONNE: I don't know exactly.

HENRI: Is he in Germany? Is he in France?

YVONNE: The letter was sent from France.

HENRI: That means nothing. He might have given it to someone.

YVONNE: I think he must have escaped.

HENRI: Obviously. Jerry didn't present him with a free travel pass for a European holiday.

YVONNE: No need to be angry. It's not my fault.

HENRI: And when he comes back and hears his best friend's been knocking off his wife he'll cut off my balls. (*Pause.*) Tell me exactly how it happened.

YVONNE: Someone knocked early, about an hour after you left.

HENRI: Who?

YVONNE: I promised not to say.

HENRI: Alright. Then what.

YVONNE: He told me Jules made a run for it ten days ago with three others. The other three...

HENRI: The other three what?

YVONNE: They set the dogs on them.

HENRI: And Jules?

YVONNE: Was always a fast runner.

HENRI: Go on.

145

YVONNE: He's coming back any day. I'm to expect him but to keep stumm.

HENRI: Hell and damnation.

YVONNE: He's my husband after all.

HENRI: Thanks for the reminder.

YVONNE: What am I to do?

HENRI: I need you Yvonne.

YVONNE: And what about him? Doesn't he need me?

HENRI: Not like I do. (*Kisses her passionately.*) I can't bear the thought of him holding you like I hold you. I can't bear the thought of you and he...

YVONNE: Stop it Henri. Stop it. Imagining that is impossible now.

HENRI: How so? He's your husband. It's his right.

YVONNE: And my rights?

HENRI: To remain faithful to him.

YVONNE: It's you I want. He may be my husband but you're my man.

HENRI: I could be both.

YVONNE: What do you mean?

HENRI: I think you understand me.

YVONNE: What are you suggesting?

HENRI: Well we thought he was –

YVONNE: Dead.

HENRI: Yes. And just suppose we never got the message. After all the man who gave it to you doesn't exist.

YVONNE: You mean betray him?

HENRI: It's not betrayal. Imagine if the dogs had got him with the other three, we wouldn't even be having this conversation and you and I could pass before the mayor by Christmas. (*HENRI puts his hand up her skirt.*) Think about it Yvonne.

YVONNE: Oh...

HENRI: Think about it Yvonne. My sweet wife.

Scene 22
How to Kill a Woman

PIERRE, GUILLAUME, RENARD dressed as off-duty policemen.

PIERRE: The briefcase has to be empty.

RENARD: No gun.

GUILLAUME: If you're caught with a gun that's the end.

PIERRE: What's your name?

RENARD: Albert?

PIERRE: Come on, come on, we're not playing any more. Your name?

RENARD: Jerôme Toubeaux.

PIERRE: Date of birth.

RENARD: 3 March 1923.

GUILLAUME: Occupation.

RENARD: Teacher.

PIERRE: Date of birth.

RENARD: Er, 1920, 4 November.

PIERRE: (*Shouting.*) Wrong, wrong, wrong. 3 March 1923. Three three three. You a Catholic?

RENARD: Of course not.

PIERRE: What's the Trinity?

RENARD: Father, Son and Holy Ghost.

PIERRE: You're a Catholic.

RENARD: Three. I get it. 3 March 1923.

GUILLAUME: It's got to be automatic. Age, profession, place of birth.

RENARD: Easy. Maubeuge.

(*Questions are very quick now.*)

PIERRE: Father's name?

GUILLAUME: Profession?

RENARD: Teacher.

PIERRE: Father's name?

RENARD: Bernard.

GUILLAUME: Mother's name?

RENARD: Edith.

PIERRE: Date of birth.

147

RENARD: Father, Son and Holy Ghost.

(*They laugh.*)

PIERRE: I've a mission for you.

RENARD: Yes.

PIERRE: It's a tough one. Are you up to that?

RENARD: Yes.

PIERRE: It has to be done tomorrow. No later.

RENARD: I'm your man.

PIERRE: There's no going back once you've agreed.

RENARD: I said yes.

GUILLAUME: It's a woman.

RENARD: Oh. I didn't count on that.

PIERRE: You don't need to be alone.

GUILLAUME: I said I'd be there too. That way it would be easier.

RENARD: A woman.

PIERRE: Yes.

RENARD: Oh.

PIERRE: She's shopped us.

RENARD: Yes. I understand.

PIERRE: But you don't want to.

RENARD: It's not that.

PIERRE: I get the feeling you don't want to.

RENARD: Somehow it's worse.

RENARD: A traitor's a traitor.

PIERRE: It's the Catholic in you.

GUILLAUME: Father, Son and Holy Ghost.

RENARD: Holy Mary Mother of God.

PIERRE: You can't see the human being you've got to see the traitor.

GUILLAUME: She's already given names to Jerry.

RENARD: Do I know her?

PIERRE: Marie Aubrey.

RENARD: Marie Aubrey. But her husband was with us.

PIERRE: He was a miner. He got us dynamite. They shot him.

GUILLAUME: She seems to have forgotten that.

RENARD: There are three kids.

PIERRE: The kids will never know.

RENARD: How's that?

PIERRE: We'll take them on. They'll be war orphans.

GUILLAUME: We'll say both parents were killed by the enemy. Who's to know otherwise?

RENARD: I can't do it. Not a woman. A man's different. A woman is a mother.

PIERRE: She's betrayed Philippe.

RENARD: When?

GUILLAUME: This morning. They came for him at dawn.

PIERRE: It's not easy but she's got to be dealt with. We can't lose anymore. I don't know what deal she's done with them. She knows us all through the press. We can't risk any more. The Roneo's got to be got rid of. The whole press must be dismantled.

GUILLAUME: You agreed.

RENARD: I didn't know it was her.

PIERRE: Don't think of her as a woman. Think of her as a traitor.

RENARD: Yes. You're right. It's just that their flesh is different from ours.

GUILLAUME: We'll do it together. That way neither of us will know who's responsible.

PIERRE: It has to be silent. I don't want any noise. You'll use a knife. Pistols are forbidden.

GUILLAUME: Agreed.

PIERRE: Agreed?

RENARD: Agreed.

PIERRE: Tomorrow morning she goes across the ramparts to give information. That's when. (*The men shake hands.*)

Scene 23
From Theory to Practice

MARIE is crossing a field. The men catch her. She screams. They wrestle with her. She needs to have a force which almost overpowers the two men.

RENARD takes out a knife but cannot kill her. She struggles. GUILLAUME takes out a gun and shoots her.

They run away.

MARIANNE DE VICHY is watching from stage right. She sings 'Bel Ami' and drags off MARIE's body.

Scene 24
A Husband's Return

YVONNE at home listening to illegal French broadcasts from London. Someone taps. She puts the radio away. She expects HENRI. There's a haggard man at the door. She stares at him in disbelief.

YVONNE: Jules!

JULES: Can I come in?

YVONNE: Jesus Christ.

JULES: Am I that bad?

YVONNE: Come in, come in.

JULES: Let me look at you. You don't know how long I've dreamt of this moment.

(*He embraces her.*)

YVONNE: Oh Jules.

JULES: You are so lovely.

YVONNE: Are you hungry?

JULES: Is the Pope a Catholic?

YVONNE: I've bread, eggs, cheese.

JULES: Yes.

YVONNE: What?

JULES: Yes. (*Pause.*) I can't believe I'm here.

YVONNE: Nor can I.

JULES: I sent a message.

YVONNE: Yes but I could hardly believe it.

JULES: You are beautiful.

YVONNE: How did you...

JULES: Escape?

YVONNE: Yes.

JULES: Nine months. Nine long months. My whole lifetime.

YVONNE: Yes.

JULES: Did you miss me?

YVONNE: Yes.

JULES: You've not touched me.

YVONNE: It's the shock. (*She opens her arms to him.*) Nine long months not knowing where you were.

JULES: Long enough to have a child.

YVONNE: I didn't.

JULES: No.

YVONNE: How are you?

JULES: My German's improved.

YVONNE: Yes.

JULES: How are you?

YVONNE: Well.

JULES: (*Patting her bottom.*) You haven't gone hungry then.

YVONNE: It's worse in the cities. In Paris.

JULES: So they say. Your mother?

YVONNE: She's fine. Your brother?

JULES: I don't know. Disappeared. (*Cries. YVONNE holds him.*)

YVONNE: Let me put you to bed.

JULES: You talk to me as if I were your child, not your husband.

YVONNE: You need rest.

JULES: Yvonne.

YVONNE: Yes.

JULES: Do you love me?

YVONNE: You know I do.

JULES: Say it.

YVONNE: I love you Jules.

JULES: Say it.

YVONNE: I love you Jules.

JULES: How are you managing?

YVONNE: I work.

JULES: Where?

YVONNE: Aulnoye. The factory.

JULES: Keeping Jerry going.

YVONNE: I have to eat.

JULES: (*Dully.*) Oh yes.

YVONNE: You're blaming me.

JULES: No.
YVONNE: Your tone.
JULES: I'm tired.
YVONNE: You can rest here.
JULES: Not long.
YVONNE: What?
JULES: It's the first place they'll look.
YVONNE: I'll find you a safe house.
JULES: Yes.
YVONNE: We can see one another.
JULES: Yes.
YVONNE: I love you.
JULES: Do you?
YVONNE: Yes.
JULES: Is there someone else?
YVONNE: I love you.
JULES: I'd understand. It's been a long time.
YVONNE: (*Pause.*) There's nobody else.
JULES: Is that true? I heard...
YVONNE: No! You heard nothing.
JULES: You'll find me a safe house.
YVONNE: Yes.
JULES: Don't let me sleep too long.
YVONNE: No.
JULES: I love you. You're my wife aren't you?
(*He falls asleep on the chair. YVONNE looks at him.*)

Scene 25
The Factory

The next morning. Everyone is working.

HENRI: He's back, isn't he?
YVONNE: How do you know?
HENRI: I know.
YVONNE: He looks terrible.
HENRI: You don't look too good either.
YVONNE: I didn't sleep. My eyes are grit.

HENRI: What does he say?

YVONNE: Not much.

HENRI: You kill me, you really do. What did he say?

YVONNE: (*Pause.*) Not much.

HENRI: He loves you?

YVONNE: Yes.

HENRI: And you?

YVONNE: I don't know.

HENRI: Where's he going to stay?

YVONNE: I promised to find somewhere.

HENRI: He needs a safe house.

YVONNE: Where? Who?

HENRI: And us?

YVONNE: Henri.

HENRI: And us.

YVONNE: Oh for God's sake.

HENRI: You're dropping me.

YVONNE: I didn't say that.

HENRI: You're dropping me.

YVONNE: (*Half whisper.*) I can't.

HENRI: What was that?

YVONNE: I said I can't.

HENRI: What will you do Yvonne?

YVONNE: I'm in hell.

HENRI: Did you? Last night?

YVONNE: Don't be ridiculous.

HENRI: I couldn't bear to think of you and him like that.

YVONNE: Stop it. Nothing happened.

HENRI: Do you love him?

YVONNE: He's my husband.

HENRI: That's not what I asked.

YVONNE: He's my husband.

HENRI: Do you love me?

YVONNE: Yes.

HENRI: Then it's easy.

YVONNE: (*Bitterly.*) Oh yes, it's easy.

HENRI: A few words to François. That's all. And then it's
    as if nothing ever happened. You never got the message

from the man who does not exist. You never got a visit
from a man who does not exist.

YVONNE: (*Cries.*) Oh Jesus!

HENRI: I think you know what to do.

YVONNE: (*Puts her arms around him.*) Help me Henri.

HENRI: I can't. (*He releases her embrace.*) Only you can
make the decision.

(*Pause. YVONNE straightens her spine. She walks towards
FRANÇOIS.*
Slow fade.)

Scene 26
A Husband Betrayed

*Movement scene played at the same time as the factory scene where
everyone is working on the machinery.*

MARIANNE DE VICHY is watching in the shadows.

*HENRI is asleep. Two men stand behind him. They lift him from
the chair before he can properly wake up. They beat him and then
take him away. He shouts one word: 'Yvonne'.*

*YVONNE stops her action for a moment, looks out in to space and
then resumes her work.*

Scene 27
The Doctor's Check Up

*The CHIEF OF POLICE is present as the DOCTOR visits the
brothel for the prostitutes' weekly venereal disease check-up. The
DOCTOR sits them on chairs. Turns their backs to the audience.
Opens their legs and inspects between their legs. The CHIEF OF
POLICE looks on with obvious interest.*

DOCTOR: No problems today Monsieur le Commissaire.

COMMISSAIRE: Thank you, doctor.

(*DOCTOR still has his head between the legs of one woman.*)

DOCTOR: But Josephine is a little too red down here. Business good lately?

COMMISSAIRE: How's your wife doctor?

DOCTOR: Always tired. You know, women after a certain age.

JOSEPHINE: Business good? It's never been so good since the occupation. I'm exhausted.

COMMISSAIRE: I'm sorry to hear that. (*To the DOCTOR.*) Please convey my best wishes to Madame for a speedy recovery.

DOCTOR: (*Still between JOSEPHINE's legs.*) A little fissure of the vaginal tissue here, nothing serious.

JOSEPHINE: It's non-stop. And it's not just Jerry. I don't know what's come over everyone. They just can't get enough.

DOCTOR: Commissaire, did I ever tell you about the man who won a free trip to Paris at a village fair. Without his wife of course.
Well he goes to Pigalle and sees a pretty girl. 'How much?' he asks, 'Three hundred thousand francs.' The man nearly dies with shock. 'Three hundred thousand francs. I don't earn that in a year!' He goes down a seedier street and sees another girl. 'How much?' 'Ten thousand francs.' 'Ten thousand francs. I don't earn that in a month!' Finally he goes up to another girl. She doesn't look too fresh, but what the hell. 'Well,' he asks her, 'how much for half an hour?' 'Fifty francs,' she says. They go back to her grubby little room and he lifts up her skirt. She opens her legs and he sees something running about.
'Oh God, you've got crabs!' he yells moving away fast. 'Well,' she says, 'for fifty francs, what do you expect? Dublin prawns?'
(*JOSEPHINE gets up in disgust.*)

JOSEPHINE: Oh please. I've just had my lunch.
(*The COMMISSAIRE pats the DOCTOR on the back.*)

COMMISSAIRE: Oh that's good, I must remember that one. What did you expect – Dublin prawns!!

DOCTOR: Now girls, what about a glass of champagne before we go?

Scene 28
The Funfair

MARIANNE DE PARIS and MARIANNE DE VICHY are sparring.

MASTER OF CEREMONIES: Roll up, roll up, ladies and gentlemen. Oh dear, our German guests have lost at Russian roulette. But let's not worry here in our wonderful country L'Hôtel de France. Here come our American cousins! Over-sexed, overpaid and over here. But ladies and gentlemen, before they arrive, hurry, hurry, hurry, make a fortune on our black market stall. Postwar anonymity guaranteed. Don't forget, your neighbour's empty belly is your passport to great personal wealth.
See these hungry people. All you have to do is feed them. Sell your butter, eggs and cheese at the highest possible price and jackpot! In the Black Market Game protection against competition guaranteed. All you've got to do is keep your mouth shut.
But don't worry. All names of collaborators and black marketeers will be held by our future governments in sealed vaults. Make thousands and never be caught! Isn't that good news ladies and gentlemen!
And now, on this lovely June day of nineteen-hundred and forty-four we've opened a new booth. Ladies and gentlemen. It's called the Resistance Stall! You just give your name and you too can be a brave member of the Resistance. Ladies and gentlemen, don't forget, it's always best to be on the winning side!
(*MARIANNE DE VICHY is knocked out by MARIANNE DE PARIS. The crowd roars with pleasure.*)

Scene 29
The Brothel

Music is 'Carnet du Bal' by Marcel Cariven and Orchestra. Waltz.

COMMISSAIRE: Well girls, how about it?
JOSEPHINE: Count me out. You heard the doctor.

COMMISSAIRE: What about you Chantal? (*CHANTAL ignores him and dances with one of the girls.*

He smacks MARIE on the bottom and then takes her upstage left. The others waltz downstage from right to left. A little girl (daughter of one of the prostitutes) stands watching the COMMISSAIRE and MARIE. The COMMISSAIRE pushes MARIE down on all fours and fucks her from behind. It should be done to humiliate her. He grunts like a pig. She pretends to enjoy it and then looks at her watch. The effect should be disturbing and absurd.

There is knocking at the door. A POLICEMAN enters. Action continues as before during dialogue.)

POLICEMAN: Excuse me for disturbing you Monsieur le Commissaire.

(*He shakes hands with everyone. COMMISSAIRE ignores him and carries on fucking.*

Bowing his head respectfully to MARIE.) Mademoiselle. Monsieur le Commissaire, I must tell you that outside it's getting worse.

There's more than two thousand of them screaming for blood. They are threatening to go in to the Caserne Joyeuse. They say they don't care what de Gaulle says. They say they want vengeance on the two collabos, Pinguet and Jacquet. Their leader Prosper is about to go in there. God knows what's going to happen. There's going to be bloody revolution. And there's a kangaroo court. All night they've been bringing up names. It's so hot in there, there's so many people inside the town hall that the paper's peeling off the walls. And Commissaire, your name's come up. They say you had a resistance man shot for stealing coal from a German wagon. They say they are coming for you. They've already started looking. Don't worry I made sure I wasn't followed.

(*The COMMISSAIRE is still in action. He appears to take no notice.*)

MARIE: To have someone shot for stealing coal is a bit much.

COMMISSAIRE: Bastards, they're all bastards. I was doing my job. What else was I to do? Filthy Communists,

filthy reds, anarchists, Jews, pederasts, the lot of them.
Filthy Communists with their sabotage. I'd have the lot
of them shot, oh… (*Crying in orgasm.*)
(*MARIE neatens her hair and dress. She gets up.*
As he buttons up his flies.) Can't a man get some relief
without being disturbed. (*To the little girl who has been
watching everything.*) Come here my lovely. Give me a big
kiss. I hope when you're a big girl you'll know how to
please a man.
(*Sounds of gunfire.*)
Let's get the hell out of here. Time to join the other side.
Paris is worth a mass, don't you think?
(*Blackout.*)

Scene 30
The Latest Cut 1944

*A WOMAN is sitting in a chair. A MAN stands behind her with a
pair of scissors as if just about to cut her hair.*

*A German SOLDIER is also present but he is in the WOMAN's
memory.*

WOMAN: The cut of 1944. You don't need shampoo or
curling tongues. This is really à la mode. In fact there's
another advantage, it costs nothing to keep neat. You can
tip the coiffeur if you want to. Him. It's always him.
Pure white him. Never fucked the wife of a comrade
away on forced labour. Never visited a good time girl
with the juices of Jerry running out of her. Oh of course.
He was in the Resistance. As soon as he knew the
Germans were beat. They all were, Cocky little men with
their feet in the shit while they shout victory.
Coco-rico!
Yes, I know them. They came to me before Jerry. When a
man's inside you you don't care if his cock is French
German or American.
But, at least with Jerry at least there's a certain courtesy.
Gnädige Frau, may I enter now?

Then he shows you a photo of Fraulein back home and you know in this corner of France you are giving the warmth of a stolen afternoon's pleasure. What does he know poor sod. He doesn't want to be here. He wants to be back home. The bastard knows he's probably going to die here.

And so what.

Didn't he kill too.

So go on, get it over with. Shoot my lovely Kraut. Shoot my lovely Frenchie. Don't forget to give Jerry one as he runs back home. Come on. Be bold my little French chocolate soldier.

Me I'm brave with these bastards. Punish the women for what the men do. If I sell my cunt then there's always a client. Who is more guilty the seller or the buyer? And does the Reichsmark stink more than the franc? Oh you make me laugh with your sense of justice.

Men came to me in the night, in the morning, in the afternoon. Tits and ass. That's all they want. Woman is just a hole where man leaves his mark in eternity.

No words. With words. Brutally. Tenderly. Meine liebe. Ich liebe dich. Words of love for an afternoon. Forgotten by night.

They used to cut off heads now they only cut hair. It'll soon grow back.

(*She puts on a headscarf. Music: 'When The Saints Come Marching In'.*)

Bonjour Yankee Soldier Boy! What do you want to give me? Nylon stockings? It's a long time since I had a good pair of stockings on me. You want to help me put them on?

(*She lifts her skirt and we hear sounds of American tanks and voices.*)

159

Scene 31
Letter from an American Soldier

American music.

This scene can be done for real or can be on tape against a dance performed by THE WOMAN WITH THE SHAVED HEAD.

AMERICAN SOLDIER: You'll never believe where I am mom. It's a town with a crazy name. Maubeuge. It's from the Latin and means something like Bad Land. It's just a ruin really but there are over three thousand Jerry prisoners here and I take night patrol, Caserne Joyeuse is where they keep them. Not that it's a place of joy. Joyeuese was some general in some other war.

Jerry doesn't say much. He's young. I guess you could say he's ashamed. The whole place is a shambles mom. Don't worry. There's no danger. And I'm not alone. There's a French boy of seventeen with me. I don't know who's more scared, him or me. No I'm kidding. Our only trouble is that we can't talk one word to one another. But we kinda speak with our hands. We try and make jokes about Jerry. He knows a few words. Gum. Corned beef. Chocolate.

I try to think back to how I was at seventeen. I mean this kid's seen it all now. He's lived more in his lousy seventeen summers than most people in a whole life. I mean out here there were a lot of guys shot. Resistance. Collaborators. And the women. You should see what they do to the women who went with Jerry. Mom they shave their heads. Sometimes they run them naked through the streets. They draw a swastika on their heads or on their breast. It's something you wouldn't do to a dumb animal. But this is Europe. It's something else over here. But the girls are real friendly. Real pretty too. We give them nylons and mom, it's as if we give them a mink coat. This guy of seventeen. His name's Pierre. That means Peter. But he's not a Catholic. No he's a Communist. I mean what did I ever know about communism at

seventeen? Don't worry mom. I'm in no danger of
turning red. I just want to do my job out here. Be a good
American. I mean people really suffered out here. The
Germans…well it's not easy to describe what they did.
You hear things out here that you just wouldn't believe
mom. Things I just couldn't put on paper. The US seems
a long way from where I am now. You know, when I'm
sitting out here, with this kid of seventeen, watching all
these Germans, it's as if I dreamed up America.
I'm going to wrap up now mom. My friend here, Pierre,
asks me to send you his greetings. He says, 'Salut à ta
mère.' So it's goodbye from Pierre who you don't know
and from your ever-loving son cos now I have to get
back to the other guys in camp. Hey mom, I miss your
pecan pie.

Scene 32
Military Court (Autumn 1944)

PROSECUTOR: You were born on the twelfth of July at
five rue Trou au Sable, Maubeuge. Your father Albert
Clément kept a bistro in rue hundred-and-forty-fifth
regiment. You married Jules Sauvage, a railway worker
in Maubeuge on 7 May 1933.

YVONNE: I wore a long champagne coloured dress. There
were six maids of honour.

(*JULES and YVONNE dance. He lifts her up.*)

PROSECUTOR: You met Henri Duclos.

YVONNE: In 1941. In May.

PROSECUTOR: Your husband Jules.

YVONNE: Was in the Resistance.

PROSECUTOR: And you too Madame?

YVONNE: No.

PROSECUTOR: Your husband was arrested for cutting
telephone lines and cables on 16 June 1941.

YVONNE: Correct.

PROSECUTOR: Were you glad to see him deported?

DEFENCE: Question is not applicable.

PROSECUTOR: You had afterall known Monsieur Duclos for a whole month.

DEFENCE: This is disgraceful.

PROSECUTOR: Monsieur Clément was immediately deported to Germany after arrest and interrogation in Gestapo headquarters in the prison at Loos.

YVONNE: Yes.

PROSECUTOR: Tell us what happened then.

YVONNE: I found work in Aulnoye.

PROSECUTOR: What sort of factory?

YVONNE: Spare parts.

PROSECUTOR: Spare parts for the German war effort.

YVONNE: I had to eat.

PROSECUTOR: Of course, Madame, you had to eat. And if you had not worked for the Germans would you have starved to death? If you had joined the Resistance would you have starved to death?

YVONNE: Of course not.

PROSECUTOR: Why didn't you join the Resistance Madame?

DEFENCE: Question inappropriate to this case. Madame Clément is not on trial for not having joined the Resistance. If so, it would be necessary to try ninety-seven per cent of French men and French women.

JUDGE: Oh let's not forget the tens of thousands who joined when they knew the war was won.

PROSECUTION: Exactly Monsieur le Juge. Now Madame Clément, your job at this factory in Aulnoye was to help in the manufacture of train wheels.

YVONNE: Yes.

PROSECUTOR: Trains which deported people to Germany.

DEFENCE: Objection. Madame Clément was not responsible for the actions of the Third Reich in occupied France.

PROSECUTOR: It was before your husband's deportation that you began your liaison with Monsieur Duclos?

DEFENCE: This is absurd. Is this woman on trial for adultery?

PROSECUTOR: We are just trying to establish facts Monsieur.

YVONNE: I was alone.

DEFENCE: Nobody is accusing you of adultery Madame.

PROSECUTOR: The liaison lasted how long?

YVONNE: I don't know. Six, nine months.

PROSECUTOR: Before or soon after your husband was deported to Germany?

YVONNE: He appealed to something deep in me. He made me feel like a woman for the first time in my life.

PROSECUTOR: Have you no sense of decency? While your husband, a man who had laid down his life so that France might be free, while Jules Clément was being tortured by the Gestapo you were betraying him with a petty collaborator Henri Duclos.

YVONNE Should I choose my lovers according to their politics?

PROSECUTOR: Yes Madame. If you lie down with pigs you come up smelling of shit.

DEFENCE: Inadmissible.

PROSECUTOR: I apologise to the court. My emotion got the better of me.

DEFENCE: There is no proof that Madame Clément betrayed her husband to the Gestapo in order to be with her lover.

YVONNE: Yes, I betrayed him. I won't lie to save my skin. I betrayed him because I didn't want him back. He turned up one night and slept in the house. I stayed awake all night considering life without Henri and I felt desolate. I felt ashamed but I wanted Jules to disappear, to get out of my life. That's the truth and I'm not going to deny it. If I'm a bad woman because of what I did then you can shoot me. I don't care. My life without Henri is meaningless anyway.

PROSECUTOR: And where is Monsieur Duclos?

YVONNE: I don't know. Paris I think. He said he'd write. That we'd pass before the Mayor.

PROSECUTOR: You plan your second marriage while your first husband lies in a German concentration camp.

(*One by one the ensemble sing 'The Song of the Partisans'. They come in from different parts of the stage and start the song at different times so that there is a strange build up of*

163

soundscape played against the following monologue which should appear fragmented.)

YVONNE: Monsieur Chenier, the butcher. How do you think he managed in this war?

Did he go hungry? No sir. One day the door was open and I saw him at his counter. And what do you think I saw? Meat? No.

Ingots. Hundreds of gold ingots. Piled high. High enough to buy ten new shops when Maubeuge is rebuilt. Look in to the banks and examine the accounts of the rich…

Scene 33
Liberation

Voice of De Gaulle proclaiming the new republic. Voice of Pathé News (or French equivalent). The whole company uses the set to show the reconstruction of the new France.

Scene 34
Reconstruction

Birdsong. While the company is 'rebuilding' the new town, a WOMAN hangs out washing on line. A little girl, young MARIANNE, skips and then runs in her garden.

MOTHER: Marianne. I'm just going inside for a moment. Be a good girl 'til I'm back.

MARIANNE: (*Skipping.*) One, two, three, what do I see…
(*MOTHER turns her back as if inside the house.*)
There's something here. A new toy. (*She picks up a buried unexploded bomb from the earth.*) Mummy, come and look at this!
(*MOTHER turns aghast.*)

MOTHER: No, Marianne, no, no!
(*Loud explosion.*
Blackout.)

ST JOAN

to Thomas Kampe

Characters

JOAN

Notes

The play was first performed in London by two Black and one Jewish/Arab actress. In Paris it was played by one Black and one Jewish/French actress. The play could be performed by a chorus of women. Structurally it has tableaux rather than scenes.

First production

ST JOAN, Laure Smadja, Yonnic Blackwood, Abbi Eniola
New End Theatre Hampstead, April 1997
Lighting Designer, Ian Watts

Production in Paris at Théâtre Atalante, May 1997
ST JOAN, Bonnie Greer, Laure Smadja

Both productions were directed by
Julia Pascal and Thomas Kampe

Joan Rabinowitch in a Taxi

I am in a taxi crossing London. It's a hot summer's
afternoon. The taxi driver is a Hindu. Tells me about
reincarnation. How you never die. After death you are
reborn. You start on the journey as an insect maybe, so
never kill a fly you never know it might have been your
father in another life and then with each lifetime you
learn something and you gain a higher consciousness
and next time round you are born as, say, a goat or a
cow and so it goes on until you are reborn as a human.
First a woman of course and then if you behave well and
live a good life then maybe a man which of course is
higher than a woman and then highest of all is a priest. It
is a hot night, I go to sleep with the window open.
Joan of Arc!
What would it be like to come back as Joan of Arc?

Joan's Dream

Domrémy
I lie in my bed at night and through the window I see
the great crossroads
that cut France and
Germany
Roads for travellers?
Roads for armies?
Here where the roads meet they form a cross
A St Andrew's cross
Under my window. A cross
Lorraine
I see a great four-headed road
Paris
Aix la Chapelle
Prague
Vienna
Domrémy lies on the brink of a boundless forest
Haunted by fairies

At night, once a year
In the summer as night falls and spirits awaken
the priest goes to the forest and reads mass to keep the
fairies' power down

Joan's Trial

(*All these voices come from her. She is both accuser and accused.*)
Do you give yourself over to the Church Militant?
Yes
You say God has ordered you to wear men's clothing
Yes
So why do you want to wear women's dress for your
death?
Do you know that Saint Catherine and Saint Margaret
hate the English?
They love those who our Lord loves and they hate those
God hates
Does God hate the English?
I don't know but I know the English will be booted out
of France! Except for those who die here

Joan Sings Mass

(*With horror.*)
The body had to be reduced to cinders and thrown in the
Seine
They dress me in a long white tunic and a tall white hat
And on it they write
'heretic
backslider
apostate
devil-worshipper'
The sound of the cart's wheels on the cobble and it's five
hundred year's humiliation as they lead me and 'witch'
they scream
I was born on the night of the Epiphany January 6th
fourteen twelve

They say that on that night the cocks in the countryside
crowed with unusual persistance and the villagers
experienced an inexplicable sensation of great joy
'France will be saved by a Virgin!'
People spoke of other marvellous events. The singing of
the the cocks, this *cantus gallorum,* seemed to have a
singularly prophetic quality.
And when the cock crows three times he will say…
The body had to be reduced to cinders and thrown in the
Seine
On the Wednesday
After Trinity Sunday
I was guarded by eight hundred spearmen and led to a
platform of a great height
constructed of a wooden billet supported by occasional
walls and lathe and plaster and traversed by hollow
spaces in every direction
For the creation of air currents
The man who orders my death
the Bishop of Beauvais dies on soft down
and
I
I
I in a fire upon a scaffold

Joan Takes a Trip to Paris

It is a coolish summer, and, as usual, in August, Paris is
empty of Parisians, only the tourists fill the streets to
marvel at the Arc de Triomphe, the Eiffel Tower, the
Champs Elysées and the Folies Bergères. The Americans
gasp at the beauty of the old world, its heavy heavy
history, its tiny windy streets or great tree-lined
boulevards. Here there are no blocks, no grid system, no
sky-scrapers. Here is Europe! Here is culture! Here is
the cradle of civilisation. And the women! So chic. So
elegant. So beautifully made-up. Even the shop assistants
like a cover-girl and in the throat-tugging beauty of

171

Paris, the Americans feel like Europe's country cousins in their sneakers and casuals. They sense that terrible patronising glance as the Parisians hear their voices, look them over and then turn away. America is the enemy. America with its easy confidence. It's Coca Cola – Macdonald on every boulevard. America is a giant ready to swallow the delicacy that is France. But, Americans must be tolerated. (*Imitates a bourgeois racist.*) 'They bring dollars to the city which God knows we need with so much unemployment. You see we French have become the good Samaritans of the world. We've so many lazy immigrants to feed, who arrive secretly to take our money, our housing, our streets.'

It was a coolish summer and, as usual, most of the Parisians were away from the city when the Africans without papers heard they were to be rounded up. They were young. They didn't know that a previous round-up had been part of daily life here not that long ago. They didn't know that in the Parisian houses which once belonged to the Jews, the French now eat and sleep without a thought of the dispossessed. The Africans are Catholics. The Jesuits gave them the French language and their man on the cross so it was natural that the Church was where they would hide. 'The Church will protect you,' the Jesuits had said. And the Africans, who believed the white men, listened to those words and buried them deep in their hearts for safety. The Africans hid in the Parisian Church that summer just before the Polish Pope's first visit to Rheims fifteen hundred years after Clovis was baptised. Now there was no Clovis. No Emperor Napoleon. No de Gaulle. Now there was a statesman called Charles. Pasqua. Like Pascal. Like Pascal lamb. Like Easter. Charles Pasqua made the laws that lifted the axe that broke the doors of the Church in Paris where the Africans were hiding. And all over France, from the Côte d'Azur to the Normandy beaches the people were horrified when they read their thin summer newspapers (for all the journalists were on holiday and so there was little news reported) but those who read were full of disgust.

How could the police dare to break the doors of a Church?

This government is not to be trusted. Is there no respect? (*Imitates a National Front sympathiser.*)

'The blacks don't cause trouble like the Algerians but even so what right have they to be here with their families always more and more children and expecting us to help all the time? France can't feed everyone who comes knocking on their door, Jean-Marie Le Pen, well, I don't agree with everything he says but you know he has a point about all these people who come here and take our bread…'

This time they don't put the people into a large stadium called Drancy and on to trains going East. This time they put them on planes. Africa. But few people notice. Paris is on holiday.

And anyway it was a difficult year for the President. Jack the Lad. President Jack went to see the Pope as soon as he was elected. Bless me father for I have…we have… dared to cut off the head of a king and the Church but we…I mean I will…forgive France?

And the Pope smiles and thanks God again for his goodness in delivering the world from the communist beast and in to his mind comes another President. François. François. Always loyal to the great hero of Verdun – Pétain. Always lays a wreath on his grave each eleventh day of the eleventh month. Great François. Great old man of the Left born in to the Right, always served his country, served Pétain, even in those days when the Nazi beast spread his shadow on the great land that is France, great François who served the Marshall who served the Nazi so well they gave him a medal and

then he changed sides to serve the Resistance a great
Socialist and a great son of the Church, oh the double
face of the man but what a man. Great François who
even at his death celebrated not one but two funeral
masses to show his fidelity to the holy Church. Great
François, honoured by the Jewish Archbishop of Paris in
Notre Dame, Our Lady pray for us sinners now and at
the hour...and there in his home town a second mass for
his wife and his mistress to attend with his legitimate and
less legitimate children but forgive him God for he
forgives himself

Joan Returns to her Dream

Where am I?
Rouen?
Domrémy?
Domrémy stands upon the frontiers and, like other
frontiers produces a mixed race
Bastard
Charles the Bastard
I crowned him king
in Orleans

Joan on the Battlefield

To kill an Englishman is to liberate La France. The first
is always the worst they say. The first. He comes towards
me. He thinks I am a young man of course. I withdraw
my sword and plunge it into his soft gut. The surprise on
his face just before the blood spurts from his stomach
and then he lifts his sword, where does he find the
strength with all that blood, so hot you could almost feel
it burning? He lifts his sword. Will he kill me? No the
arm falls. God forgive me it's for the love of France.

Joan Studies European History

JOAN: Syn

JOAN: chron

JOAN: icity

JOAN: Charles

JOAN: de Gaulle

JOAN: King of the Gaulles

JOAN: The Gaulles? Is that the French?

JOAN: Yes that's why they smoke Gaulloises

JOAN: Ha ha ha

JOAN: The Franks are the French

JOAN: Then who are the Gaulles?

JOAN: A group who were there before the Franks

JOAN: Who were the Franks?

JOAN: Came from Germany. Their first king was Clovis, king of the Franks, that is the French

JOAN: Wait

JOAN: If he was a Frank that is a German, how could he be a French king?

JOAN: Clovis?

JOAN: Yes, the one the Pope went to honour in Rheims in 1996

JOAN: Honour him? Why?

JOAN: To celebrate the one thousand five hundred years since Clovis was baptised a Christian so making France the eldest daughter of the Church

JOAN: So this was when France was born?

JOAN: Well yes and no

JOAN: What do you mean yes and no?

JOAN: The name 'France' does not exist yet

JOAN: I'm beginning to get confused

JOAN: It's quite easy England which is made up of Angles and Saxons and Jutes was really German this is not to forget the invasions by the Norsemen and the existence of the Celts. Romans of course had to invade to build roads and give us central heating. Then came the Normans who were a sort of elite caste, speaking French

175

JOAN: Who originally came from an elite caste of Germans speaking German who then became French

JOAN: And what about the Goths, Visigoths and the Ostrogoths?

JOAN: And the Vandals?

JOAN: And the Huns?

JOAN: And the Arabs?

JOAN: That was later. Charles Martel defeated them at Poitiers in 732.

JOAN: And the Crusades?

JOAN: Later, much later. Christians go to Jerusalem killing Moslems and Jews.

JOAN: And then they kill one another?

JOAN: Later. St Bartholomew's Day Massacre

JOAN: Huguenots to England? That's why England is Protestant?

JOAN: No that's another story.

JOAN: If the first French king was a German speaker called Clovis and the idea of France did not yet exist, what are we talking about? What is this French nation?

JOAN: Like the English who descend from those Norman kings and now have an English queen whose family is German and whose husband is Greek

Joan at the French Revolution

To kill a king...to cut off his head...is to cut off God's head. (*Scream.*) And when you kill the King you kill God?

I anointed a king. I created a king. I am the virgin mother of kings.

(*A voice from within her. JOAN's voices are the voice of the National Front.*)

La France aux français

France for the French

Joan Visits an Art Gallery

Look! There's a painting of me chasing the prostitutes
away from the French army. Of course I chase them.
There's work to be done. Men always having to jiggle
their dicks around what good is that when there's an
enemy to fight? And women always prepared to sell
their fannies. Sex? Me I always give it away. Give and
you shall receive, isn't that what the bible says?

Joan Meets the Dauphin

Is there someone there?
(*To audience.*) Who is that? Who? Charlie?
Charles le Dauphin?
The king in waiting?
In London we've got a Charlie in waiting too
I'm Joan. Joan Rabinowitch. Call me Joan Robinson for
short. (*Ironic.*) Like Robinson Crusoe.
You dreamed of me coming to crown you? No I'm
dreaming you. You're not dreaming me.
Where am I from?
Domrémy?
No I've been to Paris. I've been to Lille. I've even been
to Rouen. But Domrémy. No. I'm from London that's the
capital of oh yes of course you know Charlie there's
something I want to ask you. The English who are
attacking you, aren't they descendents of the Normans
who attacked England in 1066 and now they've come
back home. They're sort of French Prussians aren't they?
I mean how can you take offence when you're all the
same people? French. (*Beat.*) Ignorant, that's ignorant is
it? Well to hell with you. If you're so damned clever why
have you been Dauphin for seven years?
Me?
Oh you noticed? (*She stokes her own face.*)
Yes that's right.
No not Africa. At least not for a long time. The East End.

Charlie. Listen. If I crown you it's going to be one
terrible mistake. For you. For me. Certainly for me.
They're going to burn me. A mistake. For France. For
England. For the whole world. You see if I crown you,
France will grow in confidence and she will need
lebensraum. Expansion.
If you become king you'll conquer
Jerusalem,
Egypt,
Naples,
Palermo,
Acre,
Hungary.
If you become king then everything will be set for the
penetration of Africa
Cyprus,
Armenia.
Indochina
Vietnam
Today the Americans talk about Vietnam where Dien
Bien Phu is your Waterloo.
Algeria! What beauty! Who could fail to love it, a
paradise of Moslem, Christian and Jew in one brief
moment under the glory of French rule. But the moment
was stolen. And oh the pain of giving it up. Like cutting
off your right hand, or having it severed.
IN
DEEP
END
ENCE
independence – independence from France – how could
anyone wish it? Those men take back their land back
and force us out of heaven. They send their grandsons to
walk French streets, they walk on rainy French
pavements. Why should we give them jobs or welcome
them to our land when they kicked you out of theirs, or
was it theirs?
Oh the beauty of the desert. Dazzling white light sand
shifts oh the thrill of that moving beige

JOAN: (*Voice inside her. A memory.*) Slave chateaux

JOAN: Slave castles

  Bristol. Liverpool. Nantes. La Rochelle. Bordeaux

JOAN: Today the black Americans return to see...

Joan Goes to Theresienstadt

JOAN: I walk through Terezin. Theresienstadt near Prague.

JOAN: Theresienstadt

JOAN: Marie – Thérèse's city a city of barracks perfect

JOAN: for housing Prague's Jews before their journey to

JOAN: Look! Black and white films of 'happy' Jews smiling
  for the Red Cross

JOAN: (*At the stake.*) Show me the cross before I die

JOAN: An English soldier shows me the cross

JOAN: A city which is completely square

JOAN: And in these places where the Jews of Prague die

JOAN: Today stands a huge cross on the wall.

JOAN: (*At the stake.*) Show me the cross before I die

JOAN: And in these slave chateaux

JOAN: Where we were ripped from our land

JOAN: There is still the sign of a cross on the wall

JOAN: (*At the stake.*) Show me the cross before I die.

Joan Returns to See the Dauphin

Charlie!

There's something else I have to tell you. Not only am I
black but I'm also a Jew.

A Jew. That's right. J for Jesus. E for England. W for
Woman.

Jew like Mary.

Holy Mary Mother of God pray for us sinners...

I'm what you call Black British.

Mother from Jamaica, father from the East End. My
father was from Russian Jewish stock. Or Polish. Or
Lithuanian. Depends when the borders were drawn.
Anyway he was from the East where the Angel of Death

speaks Yiddish. My father? Mr Rabinowitch now Robinson. Wanted to get even with his family. They didn't want him to marry a shicksa so he married a West Indian. You can imagine how that pleased them! Moses was an African. Moses marched the Jewish slaves out of Egypt and it took him forty years. Now even on foot that's a long time because Egypt is just down the road from the Promised Land. *

JOAN: Why forty years?

JOAN: So that the old slaves would die and a new generation would be born. So that the memory of slavery would be forgotten

Joan Returns to See the Dauphin

(*In the French production Arab / Jewish JOAN was wrapped in an old army coat like a drunken unknown soldier. Behind her, black JOAN played the accordian. This tableau is JOAN of Arc as a tramp discussing history with Charles the Dauphin.*)

JOAN: No! No! No! I won't. I won't crown Dauphin in to king. No! Carry on living a peaceful life. I don't kill anyone. You don't hand me over to the English. France dissolves into anarchy and republicanism and the Church disappears! There will be no money to build ships to steal blacks for slavery in the colonies, no aristos, no need for the French Revolution, no overdressed doll Marie Antoinette – let-them-eat-cake

---

* *There is a second version of this speech, for a Black American JOAN:*
'I'm what you call Black American Jewish British. Father from Chicago. Mother from London's East End. My mother was from Russian Jewish stock. Or Polish. Or Lithuanian. Depends when the borders were drawn. Anyway she was from the East where the Angel of Death speaks Yiddish. My mother Miss Rabinowitch, now Mrs Robinson, her parents, they didn't want her to marry a goy, so she married a black GI! You can imagine how that pleased them. Moses was an African. Moses marched the Jewish slaves out of Egypt and it took him forty years. Now even on foot that's a long time because Egypt is just down the road from the Promised Land.'

dictatorship, no Waterloo, no re-establishment of the
heads rolling under the guillotine, no Napoleonic
monarchy, no Commune, thousands will not be
murdered, generations of men will live rather than
blood-soak the soil of France, no-one dies for Alsaçe
Lorraine names like Ypres and Mons will be merely
towns with beautiful Flemish architecture, the Somme,
Verdun and Flanders fields bring no poppy day, no
monuments *dulce et decorum est*
pro patria mori
no military bands no Rule Britannia
No Vichy. Pétain, Hitler's friend who loves Joan of Arc,
Joan still loved today by the man who wants to boot the
foreigners out
Le Pen
Pétain Le Pen – send-the-immigrants-back-to-their-own-
country
Algeria was La France and now he says La France has
become Algeria,
(*JOAN sings. This is the song of the French troops in Algeria
during the Algerian war of the 1960s.*)
C'est nous les Africains qui revenons de loin
Nous revenons des colonies pour défendre le pays
Nous avons laissé la-bàs nos parents nos amis
Car nous avons au coeur une invincible ardeur
Et nous voulons porter haut et fier
Le beau drapeau de notre France altière
Et si quelqu'un venait à y toucher, à y toucher
Nous serions là pour mourir à ses pieds
Battez le tambour
Pour nos amours
Pour le pays
Pour la patrie
Vive les Africains!

Joan's Second Trial

(From now on the historical imperative starts to slip in to the action. These inner voices can be stuttered, spluttered or filled with pain but they should never be easy.
JOAN is both judge and suspect.)

JUDGE: How did Saint Michael appear? Was he naked?

JOAN: You think God's got time to buy him clothes?

JUDGE: You are on trial Joan because you are a witch

JOAN: My voices are real they are not witchcraft

JUDGE: ...women talent for sorcery...original sinners. Who took the apple from Satan?

JUDGE: Don't be smart...the devil...women's clothes... men's clothes... (*A terrible laugh.*) ...give men dreams of being king...tempting men with your smells...fawn-ick-at-ress [fornicatress] what...devil? Fornicating in the woods with the beast with a tail...entering in to men's...dreams...root you out...pollute...filthy thing between your legs...devour them with your insides... children die...drink their blood for your rites...suddenly taken ill...strike at decent...

Joan's Several Worlds Intermingle

When they burn a body in a coffin the skeleton jumps up with the shock of the heat. Bang! They lit Mrs Ghandi on the banks of the Ganges and I wanted to shout no, don't burn her body, a woman's body cannot be burnt like that, I don't know, I don't know what to do with it but burning no it seems terrible, the pain, yes I know she's already dead but can you be sure she does not feel who can tell? All dressed in white funeral not like us they dressed me in white for the stake.

Oh Jesus Mary and Holy St Joseph I'm burning!

I put my finger through the candle in the church, licking it first so it wouldn't burn.

'Witch.' Am I a witch?

'The Lord is my shepherd, I'll not want, he leadeth me to lie in green pastures'

Sing to me grandmother before I sleep. Why do you
place a chair by the bed?
In case I slip out on to the floor and hurt myself.
The English soldier on the field, his brains just spill out
Can you smell my flesh burning
My fat
My skin
My bones?
In Auschwitz, they say women take longer to burn

Joan Considers Sainthood

I am a saint because I saved France from the English.
But a real saint, a saint worthy of the name, would have
stood at the ramp as the trains arrived, as the orchestra
played Strauss a real saint would shout 'get away, take
their guns and kill them because they are already
digging the pits for your bodies'. A real saint would have
stood on the African shore and sunk the boats waiting to
steal the people from their land. Where was the Joan of
Arc to stop the holocaust of Black and Jew?

Joan Trains for Battle

The sword is heavy at first. I train myself in the cold
snowfields of Lorraine with the wolves howling, train
myself to be hard like a man. My mind is so strong. My
will can pass through centuries. Why can't I go back to
just before and stop it happening?
There is always that moment at the beginning of the day
before I remember. Before I see a black man hanging
from a tree, his penis stuck in his mouth while a white
mob yelps in joy. The British Tommies vomit in Belsen
as they shovel the legs and breasts and ribs into pits.
What's hell? It is the beast with the large brain that
teaches hell its business.
Riding high on a horse at first frightened to fall and I
fall, many times, that moment when you feel yourself

spinning through air and all you can smell is the
thudding dry odour of your own skull and then you
mount again, the cold, whinnying horse receives my
weight like a lover, heavy but necessary then we go
faster and faster so that the cold wind in my lungs
freezes me from inside.

Joan Sleeps in the Barn with the Men

My banner is heavier than my sword with Jesus Maria
painted in bold, higher, higher show your colours Joan
woman-man, no long hair, no sex and when they sleep
with me in the barns at night I can smell the men and
their want, I smell them hardly able to control
themselves at the female amongst them and I close my
eyes and pray to St Michael and then it is morning and
the men's smell is less only the smell of the horses and
their manes fill me. Still a virgin.
One more day a virgin
Send the English back to England!
Drive the foreigner out!
Crown the Dauphin!
No. Don't crown!
He wants me drowned. My own father
He wants me drowned. My own father
He wants me drowned. My own father
For riding with the men
His daughter drowned like a new-born kitten! Tie my
body with a weight and down and down
I who drove out the prostitutes
The Lord is my Shepherd
I'll not want
He leadeth me
The Lord is God
I shall have no other gods before thee
Honour thy...I love Mary and Jesus and Saint Catherine
and Saint Michael and Saint Margaret
They say I am a strumpet

a whore
a slut
a drab
a trollop
To go with the men
They say I am with child
(*Shouts.*) N-e-v-e-r
No man between my legs
Never
They foul my name here on
French soil
Every grain of soil French not English
Dirt everything reduced to dirt
To them woman is dirt
And I the maid the pure maid of France
Charles my king, don't abandon me
Don't let them take me. I ride with the men, I go as I
please. I ride high and proud with the smell of battle in
my nostrils, the smell of death, the smell of the English
dying all around me and you crowned king with the
smell of the holy incense in my nostrils Ave Maria
Holy Mary Mother of God pray for us sinners now and
at the hour of our death

VOICE: Crown the Dauphin

JOAN: No

VOICE: Go to Orléans leave Domrémy, leave your mother,
your father, your brother
Honour that thy days may be long in the land of Canaan

VOICE: Leave Lorraine, go save France

VOICE: France must be saved by a maid

VOICE: France must be saved by a virgin

VOICE: France must be saved by you

VOICE: Drive out the foreigner

JOAN: Who are you? Tell me who you are?

INNER VOICE: St Michael

INNER VOICE: St Margaret

INNER VOICE: St Catherine

INNER VOICE: Drive out the infidel, the heathen the anti-
Christ

INNER VOICE: (*More modern – JOAN must struggle with today's voices.*) Drive out the blacks
INNER VOICE: Drive out the Jews, the moneylenders, the Christ-killers
INNER VOICE: Drive out the Arabs
INNER VOICE: Save France
JOAN: I'm a girl, how can I do that?
INNER VOICE: Stop being a girl
VOICE: Be a warrior
VOICE: Be a knight!
INNER VOICE: Cut your hair, wear men's clothes, be like a man
JOAN: And alone with men, what will become of me?
INNER VOICE: We will protect you

Joan at the Stake

(*Bells ring.*)

I can smell my own death. In front of everyone in the square in Rouen high high up and the soldier shows me the cross and then the blackness of the flames and I'm coughing and the smell of my own flesh burning is sickening so I vomit like Tommy in Belsen and I'm singing Ave Maria – Jesus help me – and I'm coughing with the smoke and choking on my own vomit the pain through all my body the burning screaming pain in my flesh oh the cruelty of it all. All the world sees me burning. They burn a cross on the lawn, a flaming cross to frighten the people, no you can't live here, we burn your garden, your house and soon we will burn you and my hair is on fire and my lashes on fire and my small precious breasts no-one ever touched burnt to nothing and my belly-never-caressed all ashes and between my legs where no-one ever was nothing and my eyes burnt out nothing but the raw sockets.

But I can still see! God help me, how is it I can still see and they come for me and they show my burnt burnt body to the crowd to show them that I really am a

woman and not a witch or a devil or a dragon in
disguise, they show me to the world me who no one ever
saw naked oh the shame of what they do to me.

Joan at her Grandmother's Death

My grandmother, my Jewish grandmother. I watch her as
she is dying. Old white haired white skinned old lady do
you know who I am? You are gently rocking in the arms
of a black nurse. A big Jamaican cradling a little Yiddel.
'I'm a heavy baby,' you laugh at me. How can you laugh
when you know you are dying?
Grandmother? Do you know me? White woman I am
your flesh.
See me.
Don't look at me as if I am the nurse's child.
You die and they cover the mirrors with sheets so the
Angel of Death will not be seen when I look in the glass.
A man sits on a low stool, his face unshaven. A woman
sits next to him. My Jewish father and my Jamaican
mother.
Africa and Egypt together in the European House of
Death.

Joan Takes a Train to Paris

The train speeds past Compiègne and towards Paris
Nord. I look up in to the sky and there are two different
cloud waves. It's a contradiction. How can the wind blow
east and west at the same time?
It must be a trick of light
Or a trick of speed.
Yes that's it. I'm time travelling in the rain
I see pyramids of grit piled high brown fields of corn
cobs already stripped ready to feed prime steaks onward
and onward high speed past marshland and men with
guns on their shoulders
onward past tiny well-kept cemeteries and then large

ones where there is no soil, only grit and, on the graves,
nothing but chrysanthemums
All Souls
Toussaint
All Saints
The fast moving sky is blue
And grey
And white
A confetti of leaves hits the window and the nearer we
get to Paris the yellower the leaves
Coal wagons wait
For what?
The Poles who came to tear coal from the earth are dead
in the cemeteries we just passed
The Poles are now French
But still Catholic
Porte d'Orléans
Villejuif
Jews' town
Verdun in the metro
An old Armenian plays a wooden instrument with
strings
A large picture of a white couple kissing – elle rencontre
l'homme de sa vie
A poster. A woman opens her mouth to suck the end of a
gun
'Make your own hard core video'
I chase the prostitutes
Give and you shall receive
Out in to the winter sunlight down the Rue de Rivoli
Money!
To the dead of the Second War. To the dead of Indo-
China. A plaque
And then opposite the Tuilleries Gardens there I am!
Gold!
But I'm gold!
Completely gold
And my horse!

Gold too
An African tourist passes
He looks up at me
Curiously
I'm in the first district
Le premier arondissement
Near la rue d'Algers
The road called Algiers
I'm in la Place des Pyramides
When we were slaves in Egypt I helped build the
Pyramids before we wandered for forty years
Golden with my back straight and proud on my horse
Golden with my right arm high
Holding my banner high high high
Suddenly there is a hot sun shooting through the wind
May. Mary's month. May the first
I am not the only one on a horse
There are others
Knights
Men on horses. I can smell the horses
Knights. Who are they?
And the crowd all around them
wide ribbons around their bodies
crossing between their breasts
Blue, white and red – what does it mean?
'*La France aux français*, France for the French'
And the smell of them is putrid even from up here high
on my horse
They come towards me honouring me
But I don't want their honour I don't like their smell
There's another smell
Merguez. Spiced sausage from Algeria. Men with
moving stalls are selling spicy sausages to the men with
shaved heads
To the knights on horseback
But I am above them all
Proud and gold only my brain is alight and the knights
their breath, I can smell their filthy breath

And the men with shaved heads wear big boots
And in the midst
A young black man
They are pushing him
They are carrying flags
Blue, white red. What does it mean?
Pro-life
What does it mean? Why are they hurting that man?
They jostle him and he is running
And I watch frozen golden on my golden horse
I am burning and frozen, my brain is alight and his
breath becomes my breath
And they chase him, the knights on their horses and the
men with shaved heads are running
And the crowds with their flags
My gold starts to melt!
My gold from Africa
It melts and all I can feel is the heat of my brain
burning, my will burning and the flesh of my horse
warms against mine
he jumps down in to the square
and we follow the crowd as they push the young man
past the Tuilleries Gardens
past the Louvre with all its treasures
and the pyramid that Jack built
onward and onward until my breath is freezing in my
lungs with the pain of the effort
onward and onward over the bridge
over the Seine
onward and onward past Notre Dame
Our Lady pray for us sinners NOW!
Onward and onward until I think we'll never catch up
with them
I'm trotting
I'm cantering
I'm galloping
And I see him. They are pushing him hard and his face
is panic

And I'm digging my heels in to his flesh to make him
gallop faster
Until I'm almost level with them
Level with him
I'm right behind you
I smell the sweat of fear
On towards the river
I follow picking up speed until all my limbs are fire and
the gold melts leaving trails of liquid all along the street
I'm chasing the knights
I'm chasing the man
and I'm there between the black man and the white
crowd
his hot breath of terror rises up to me and I say
Jump!
Venez! Sautez!
Jump up to me
Jump! Venez! Allez!

(*Blackout.*)